THE HUNTING OF FORCE Z

The Hunting of Force Z

The brief, controversial life of the modern battleship,
and its tragic close with the destruction of the
'Prince of Wales' and 'Repulse'.

RICHARD HOUGH

WHITE LION PUBLISHERS
London, New York, Sydney and Toronto

First published in the United Kingdom by
Collins, 1963

White Lion edition, 1974

ISBN 0 85617 335 5

Printed in Great Britain by
Biddles Ltd., Guildford, Surrey,
for White Lion Publishers Ltd.,
138 Park Lane, London W1Y 3DD

Contents

Illustrations

Between pages 128 and 129

Acknowledgments are due to the following for permission to reproduce the illustrations in this book: Plates 1 and 2 and the drawing on page 18 (all from *British Battleships*), the Executors of the late Dr. Oscar Parkes, O.B.E., ASS.I.N.A.; Plate 3, the United States Navy Department; Plates 4-11, the Controller of H. M. Stationery Office; Plate 12, London Express News and Feature Services.

1 "Nervous As Cats" *

Beneath the coastal waters of the Far East lies the rusting, weed-shrouded wreckage of ten great men-of-war, dispatched from Europe in abortive attempts to halt by the threat of their presence the advance of Japanese militarism. Eight are Russian and went to the bottom in 1905; the other two are British and were sunk thirty-six years later. There is a strange similarity in the rôles of these ships, in the preliminaries to combat, and in the effect of the ships' destruction. Both in 1905 and 1941 the battle was swift, bloody, and wholly decisive.

Survival for these European fleets depended on their reaching base without being sighted and engaged by the enemy. Combat meant almost certain destruction. Both Admiral Zinovy Petrovitch Rozhestvensky and Admiral Sir Tom Phillips recognised the diminishing chances of escaping catastrophe the nearer they approached their enemy. Both fleets were supported by good fortune until within a few hundred miles of security.

The Russian fleet, after a tempestuous and bizarre voyage of 18,000 miles, was within 600 miles of its base, and had been successful in evading the enemy until concealing sea mist and low cloud had suddenly opened up,

* Vice-Admiral Sir David Beatty writing on the state of the British Battle Fleet in the autumn of 1914.

and by a remote and unfortunate chance, had revealed them to a lurking Japanese scouting vessel. Within a few hours the main Japanese fleet had closed in and begun the most devastating destruction ever committed by the modern naval gun.

Thirty-six years later Admiral Sir Tom Phillips was ordered to take up an equally hazardous strategic position. New weapons of destruction and reconnaissance had meanwhile been discovered, and energetically developed by the enemy. They were aircraft of the most modern type equipped with the most powerful airborne torpedoes in the world that sought out this fleet and awaited with relish the opportunity to destroy it.

Tom Phillips's dilemma was as excruciating as had been Admiral Rozhestvensky's before him. His slender thread, too, hung on the hunting powers of the Japanese and the vagaries of the weather in the coastal waters of the Far East. Survival for the British fleet depended on its remaining unobserved during the hours of daylight on 9 December. From dawn almost until dusk, low clouds and mist obscured Sir Tom Phillips's force. Then, by the same savage mischance as before, the clouds suddenly rolled back to reveal blue skies and a Japanese scout poised high above the horizon. The commander-in-chief and his great ships were at the bottom of the ocean before another twenty-four hours had passed.

The battles of Tsu-Shima and the Gulf of Siam conveniently mark the high point and the final demise of the armoured battleship in its precarious life of eighty years, from 1861 to 1941. The destruction in December, 1941, of the *Prince of Wales* and *Repulse* in a few swift and irresistible attacks from the air marked the end of an era. It also resulted in the awakening of the most cautious traditionalist to the new order at sea. For the extreme advocates of air power, it appeared finally to decide in their favour the twenty-years-long "battleship versus bomb" controversy. For the people of Britain, who had ruled the waves long before Arne wrote his jingoistic masterpiece, and who cherished their great grey symbols of supremacy, the psychological effect was profound.

These ships had been dispatched East, in the words of Britain's Prime Minister, as "the best deterrent" and as "the one key weapon." The disaster that followed this last forlorn stroke in the old game of diplomacy by gun-boat, was to Churchill the greatest single blow of the war. And time has shown that, with her most humbling defeat of modern times, Britain lost not only two capital ships, an admiral and 840 officers and men. She also lost, and perhaps none too soon, a sense of self-esteem with manifestations that were not always attractive.

To the battles of Tsu-Shima and the Gulf of Siam can be traced the greatest revolution of the twentieth century, and the emergence of the nations of the East from material and political subservience to the West.

Before considering why wise and experienced men caused these two ships to be exposed to fatal dangers, and before describing the woeful events that led up to the Battle of the Gulf of Siam, and the sharp, valorous action itself, the modern armoured battleship has to be seen in relation to its times. Its history is brief and vainglorious; and tragi-comic are the calculations, the dogmas and the passions it caused, the influence it wielded, and above all the bloodless battles of theory it fought for most of its life against the powers of technology. Technology was always the battleship's uneasy ally, and deadly enemy. The battleship succumbed finally because, for all man's ingenuity and lavish expenditure of wealth, technology could no longer perpetuate the legend, and this weapon of war had become only a wonderful and romantic anachronism.

It would be pleasant to suggest that man for once allowed romance to enter into his defence calculations. Unhappily, this was not the case. Like most weapons of destruction created in times of peace, the first function of the battleship was to instil fear in the hearts of men. In this rôle it was as successful as the heavy bomber which joined it to form a duet of terror in the 1920s. For almost a century the threat of the armoured battleship fleet was the first instrument of power diplomacy. It supported or deposed kings and emperors, presidents, dictators, viziers and sheiks; brought about the downfall of old, and established new régimes; preserved or broke up the *status quo*, created and destroyed treaties, redrew frontiers. The ironclad fleets decided a dozen minor wars, time and again brought the great powers to the edge of conflict, and were more responsible than any other single factor for bringing about the holocaust of 1914–18.

No instrument of war has ever surpassed the battleship in its menacing grandeur, or in its disastrous ability to condition man's mind to the destruction of his fellows. And yet, for all the countless millions spent on it, for all the sacrifices, the passions, the political manipulations and pressures it occasioned, the battleship was scarcely ever used in combat. Of fleet actions with its own kind there was only one that was conclusive and decisive, and that not willingly sought by one side. For the rest, there were only bombardments of the mainly helpless and weak, ship-to-ship or squadron engagements, brief fleet skirmishes overhung by North Sea mist and the fear of decision and other weapons than the big gun, for which the battleship was a mere platform.

For all but the first twenty years of its life, the battleship was threatened by an underwater weapon that was finally to seal its fate in the Far East in 1941. By 1880 it had become apparent that a small quantity of gun-cotton exploded against the vulnerable underside and beneath the thick belt of armour, could sink or cripple a battleship costing £800,000, and perhaps tip the balance of strength in favour of an inferior enemy. The automobile torpedo provided the best means of delivering the charge. The great iron-clad's brief era of total security against all but its own kind was over and the long drawn-out contest between the battleship and its underwater foes had begun.

The torpedo's origins went back to the American War of Independence. At that time a Captain David Bushnell of Connecticut invented a form of submarine boat for "the purpose of conveying magazines to the bottom of hostile ships and there exploding them." In 1776 and 1777 Royal Navy vessels were attacked by two of Bushnell's devices linked together and allowed to drift on to their target, their fuse being operated by clockwork.

Twenty years later Robert Fulton was carrying out experiments on the Seine with a machine designed "to impart to carcasses of gunpowder a progressive motion underwater, to a certain point, and there to explode them." He got no encouragement from the French until Napoleon Bonaparte subsidised him in 1801. When attacks with his weapon against the English Channel Fleet failed, the subsidy was withdrawn and Fulton went over in disgust to the enemy in 1804. Pitt thought there was something in the idea, and although Royal Navy attacks against the French in Brest harbour were equally abortive, Fulton did succeed before a large audience in destroying the brig *Dorothea* by drifting mines. In 1806 the persistent Fulton returned to the United States and attempted to gain the support of Congress. A commission of investigation examined his drifting mine as well as his new and more elaborate harpoon and spar torpedoes, in which the explosive charge was either hurled against the hull of an enemy ship or thrust at it on the end of a long pole, both of which demanded suicidal tendencies in the operator. Congress turned Fulton down, and he retired to write a book with the spirited title of *Torpedo Warfare*.

Samuel Colt became fascinated with the idea of destroying warships by underwater explosion long before he made his name in the world of firearms. Colt successfully exploded a case of powder in New York Harbour in 1842, and for some years after this experimented with the electrical detonation of drifting mines, the underwater cable being insulated by cotton yarn in a metal case. But something a shade less haphazard than this was needed before serious results could be expected. This next stage came about as a result of the joint work of Captain John Harvey and Commander Frederick Harvey of the Royal Navy, whose torpedo was towed at some six knots, the explosion of the seventy-six pounds of rifle fine-grained powder occurring when an exposed bolt hit the bottom of a ship. This method of attack was highly regarded for a while, although the crew of the towing vessel required courage and skill of a high order to swing their weapon against the enemy at point blank rifle range. "The guiding principle of the spar torpedo," ran the instructions in a naval manual, "is that its construction and design render it necessary that wherever the torpedo goes the operator must go too."[1]

The year 1864 marks the conception of the most destructive weapon at sea until the arrival of nuclear power. In that year a Captain Lupuis of the Austrian Navy devised a self-propelling torpedo with a small charge of gunpowder fired by a pistol in the fore end, and with locomotion supplied by steam or clockwork power. This simple machine which Lupuis described as "a small fireship" was not intended to be submersible and was to be directed on to its target by ropes and guide lines. In its original form it showed little advance over what Colt among others had been doing in America, and when Lupuis offered the weapon to his government he was told to come back again when he had found a more reliable means to propel and guide it. Lupuis gave thought to these problems for a while without success, finally deciding to call in the aid of an engine works in Fiume.

The manager of this works was an expatriate Englishman from Lancashire named Robert Whitehead. Whitehead had for many years led a colourful life with machinery on the Continent since he had joined his uncle at Marseilles after serving his apprenticeship. In his early thirties he had

15

set up his own works in Milan, designed and manufactured a wide variety of industrial machinery, including special pumps for draining the Lombardy marshes, had seen all his patents annulled by the Revolutionary Government of 1848 and departed in dudgeon for Austria. He built large marine engines for the Austrian Admiralty at his new factory, including the engines for the victorious Austrian flagship at Lissa, and it was here that Lupuis came for assistance. Whitehead was then forty-one, a distinguished engineer in his field and much honoured by the Austrian Government. He turned down the offer to collaborate with Lupuis, told him his torpedo would not work, and set about building one of his own.

Whitehead worked on the weapon for more than two years, assisted only by his son and one mechanic, and produced in 1867 the prototype of the device that just fifty years later would be sinking his country's merchantmen at the monthly rate of a million tons. He had discarded both steam and clockwork as unreliable and inefficient, and manual guidance as clumsy and restricting. His torpedo carried a charge of eighteen pounds of dynamite in the nose and was powered by air compressed to 700 lb. per square inch that was contained in a chamber amidships. Its speed was about six knots, and its effective range some 300 yards. But the feature that intrigued the Austrian navy department to which it was submitted, and later caused the arrival of a sceptical but faintly anxious committee of officers from the British Admiralty, was its ability to be aimed at its target and travel towards it without further guidance beneath the surface of the sea. That the Whitehead more often went to the bottom or sprang to the surface was of small consequence; these were faults that would be cured during the period of development. When Whitehead brought two of his submersibles to England in 1870 the charge had been raised to sixty-seven pounds of gun cotton, the range had grown to a thousand yards and the running depth could be varied from five to fifteen feet. Secret and highly successful trials were carried out at Sheerness that winter, as a result of which the Government purchased the non-exclusive manufacturing rights from Whitehead for £15,000.

Other naval powers were quick to acquire their own rights to build Whiteheads, and soon the whole world was familiar with the once secret balance chamber mechanism for controlling the torpedo's running depth. The torpedo, after all, was a vessel faster than any warship in the world, was almost invisible, was incapable of destruction after dispatch on its errand, cost little more than a few heavy shells, could be used again and again in practice, and required no crew.

While the trials of the first Whiteheads were being carried out in Britain, and months before the official adoption of this weapon by the Royal Navy, the first counter steps were already being taken in the combat between surface vessels and the new underwater threat that was to continue for the remaining lifetime of the battleship. The first of these was the net. It seemed a good idea to halt the torpedo's run towards its target by putting a steel mesh net in the way, and the Admiralty became an enthusiastic exponent of the cult of the crinoline. The torpedo threat coincided with the end of masts and sails in the Royal Navy, and the exercise these had for centuries provided ships' companies. There was serious concern

The battleship HMS *Hotspur* with its torpedo net
crinoline in position

in the fleet about how to provide sufficient occupation and physical training for the men. The rigging and unrigging of net defences provided an invaluable substitute, and the smartness with which a ship performed the evolution of "out nets" on anchoring compared in importance with the manner and speed with which the main top-gallant had been unfurled by an earlier generation of seamen. Chatfield, in *The Navy and Defence*, records how nets could be dropped and swung out on their booms in ten seconds and refurled again in one minute. The apparatus for operating the nets and their booms became highly elaborate, and included thirty feet steel spars pivoted at intervals of forty-five feet, jackstays, standing lifts, guys and shackles and spectacle eyes and grummets and wire lashings, quite apart from the huge 400-pound nets themselves, complete with heavy dangling chain to retain them vertically when the ship was anchored in a current. A complex lore of net-work grew up in the service, and whole manuals were devoted to their operation and maintenance. On some of the larger battleships built in the 1880s and 1890s the total weight of the crinoline and its adjuncts was so great that it had an adverse effect on the seaworthiness of the vessel.

Although the torpedo was first envisaged as a weapon for use against battleships at anchor, when its range and mobility were increased, protection against it had also to be provided for the battle fleet at sea. To protect fully the underside of a battleship obviously demanded sacrifices in other directions, and when the first armoured double-bottoms were fitted in the late 1880s, to compensate for the additional weight the length and thickness of the side plating had to be reduced, thus making the vessel more vulnerable than ever to the heavy guns in surface actions. Other experiments in underwater protection were tried, including the placing of the coal bunkers between the ship's outer skin and her vitals, reinforced by immensely thick teak and steel plating. After 1906 an elaborate system of compartmentation below the waterline against torpedo attack became standardised in all the world's navies, and armoured bulkheads about the ship's vitals gave additional protection behind steel plating that was between seven and ten inches thick. But this measure of protection was again considered inadequate as the speed and destructive power of the torpedo were increased, and the means of delivering it became more efficient. By 1914 the idea of adding a length of padded cushioning along the battleship's waterline was gaining adherents. These excrescences, which extended anything up to fifteen feet from the ship's sides, and therefore reduced her maximum speed, were divided into air and water compartments. Like the nets and booms, the "bulge," or "blister," added nothing to the fighting efficiency nor the beauty of the ships to which they were fitted.

So much for passive defence. But within ten years of Robert Whitehead's first experiments, his torpedo was beginning to bring about fundamental changes in the battleship's gun arrangements as new means of active defence became necessary against the torpedo's first effective carrier, the torpedo boat. At first the gun defences against torpedo attack were on a modest level: a mere half dozen six-pounder quick firers, which were used also for saluting. But later more and more small calibre and light semiautomatic weapons were mounted on truncated masts as sail was dispensed with. The ten-barrel .45 and .65 Gatling, the Maxim, the Hotchkiss four-pounder machine gun, the four- and five-barrel Nordenfeldt, all with a rate of fire of between four hundred and seven hundred rounds per minute, were fitted at strategic points on the decks and bridgework and masts of battleships in order to pour in a devastating hail of fire on any light vessel approaching within their range. By the turn of the century it was not unusual for a battleship to carry as many as twenty-five or thirty light weapons for close defence.

The success of the automobile torpedo always depended on the ability of its carrier to deliver it within striking distance of the enemy and this could be accomplished either by stealth or speed. Until the turn of the century, the torpedo-boat—and its successors, the torpedo gunboat and torpedo-boat destroyer—provided the only means of

effective delivery. At first these vessels were intended primarily for swift night attack, and were accordingly painted
black. The surface-carried torpedo remained to the end a
threat to the battleship. But in the early years of the century
a sinister and revolutionary means of torpedo delivery was
devised: one that was to cause greater destruction to the
battle fleet than all the mighty naval guns in the world.

During the autumn of 1900 a curious and disturbing
report reached naval circles in Britain. It concerned the
activities of a "Holland." At that time not everyone at the
Admiralty could claim to know for sure what a Holland
was. But it appeared that in the course of manœuvres of
the United States North Atlantic Squadron, a Holland had
"made a successful attack upon the fleet at night by herself
without convoy, at a distance of seven miles from the mouth
of the harbour. She claimed to have torpedoed the flagship
of the squadron, the *Kearsage*. Lieutenant Caldwell, who
was in command of the Holland, said that he considered
that the attack was a success, because the Holland could in
all probability have torpedoed three blockading vessels
without being discovered."[2]

Long before Jules Verne's *Nautilus* inspired a number of
enterprising inventors and shipbuilders to conduct experiments with some frightening submersibles in the second
half of the nineteenth century, Fulton, Bushnell, Colt,
Nordenfeldt and others in America were working on the
problem of a craft for harbour defence combining invisibility
with offensive power. J. P. Holland, a brilliant engineer
from Ireland, who emigrated to the U.S.A. in 1873 at the
age of thirty-three, began his own experiments around
1875. He died in the month the First World War began,

just as the first British ships were going to the bottom by the torpedo carried in his invention.

John Arbuthnot Fisher, that zealous, irascible and remarkable admiral who was First Sea Lord from 1904 to 1910, and was most responsible for the expansion and modernisation of the Edwardian Royal Navy, was almost uncannily prophetic about the submarine's future potential, as he was about most new developments. Before the first batch of Hollands had even been completed for the Royal Navy, he was expressing his conviction that they would entirely alter the nature of warfare. In 1904 he was writing "I don't think it is even *faintly* realised—*the immense impending revolution which the submarine will effect as offensive weapons of war.*"[3] He gathered some strong allies in this view as the submarine was rapidly developed until it became a powerful ocean-going craft with a speed of some fifteen knots on the surface and a much greater endurance than the first Hollands. But not even Fisher and his allies could influence the general opinion of the Board of Admiralty that the submarine, like the torpedo-boat before it, was anything more than a new weapon for coastal and harbour defence, a further insurance against invasion, and an addition to the strength of the flotilla. The submarine could also be a direct hazard, of course, but had not the battleship survived other and equally over-estimated weapons, like the giant high-explosive shell, the spar and the automobile torpedo, and the mine?

From the beginning the submarine had a smaller chance than the torpedo-boat of diminishing the esteem in which the battleship continued to be held; and there was one very strong reason for this. Whereas torpedo-boat attack called up a picture of dashing courage similar to that of the cavalry charge, the submarine was generally regarded in Britain as a weapon of deceit. Treachery was the key word, and it appears again and again in the controversy that the alleged menace of the submarine aroused at this time. While Fisher was describing submarines as "the battleship of the future" and "the coming Dreadnoughts," his successor as First Sea Lord, A. K. Wilson, had termed it in 1902 as "underhand, unfair, and damned un-English." Should their crews be captured in war, he considered that they should be hung as pirates. Fisher's arch-enemy, Lord Charles Beresford, on the one hand assailed him for failing to provide sufficient light craft to screen the battle fleet at sea, while dismissing the submarine as a weapon of no consequence. "The submarine," he once scornfully described it, "is always in a fog."

It was only with the greatest reluctance that the Board permitted submarines to operate against the battle fleet on manœuvres, and the rules were loaded so strongly against them that they stood little chance of making a kill. "In one set of manœuvres," Fisher recalled, "the young officer commanding a submarine, having for the third time successfully torpedoed the hostile admiral's flagship, the young officer humbly said so to the admiral by signal, and suggested the flagship going out of action. The answer he got back by signal from the admiral was: 'You be damned!' "[3] At any time if a submarine's commander made a claim against a battleship he was obliged to come to the surface for half an hour in order to substantiate it, which did not improve his chances of survival. Referring to manœuvres involving submarines, Vice-Admiral Sir Doveton Sturdee placed on record the opinion of many

23

of his fellow flag officers when he suggested, at a War College lecture, that it was "high time we put the fear of God into these young gentlemen who lie about the North Sea attacking all and sundry without let or hindrance."

In spite of the threat of the torpedo, from 1904 the great battleship race between Britain and Germany proceeded at an ever-growing pace, consuming the wealth of the two great imperial nations, drawing them closer to cataclysm. Year by year the vessels became larger and more formidable. And yet when at last hostilities broke out, the surface maritime war of 1914-18 was primarily defensive and tremulous on both sides. So profound were the risks of failure and loss in combat, so delicately poised was the balance of power, that both British and German strategy was governed firstly by considerations of survival. It was no war for a Nelson, or a Beatty for that matter. Except for a few bombardments, a few engagements which did not affect the *status quo* or the rôles of the opposing fleets, the big guns never fired.

There were some thirty minutes of a late May evening in 1916, during four and a quarter years of war, when the main battle fleets were in sight and range of one another's big guns. Otherwise the heavy ordnance, which had for so long represented the very spirit of violent and thunderous aggression, remained a silent and hidden threat. Only among the cruisers, the flotillas and other light craft, which were allowed to risk themselves between the North Sea minefields in order to sustain the throttling blockade of the central powers, was there any sustained activity, and even the occasional opportunity to attack the enemy.

The naval mine sank ships, sometimes the light craft

clashed, but the only continuously offensive weapon was the torpedo. From the opening of hostilities to the Armistice, it remained a killer, the undisputed supreme weapon of sea warfare. The effect of the German U-boats' torpedoes on the course of the war, bringing Britain to the very brink of defeat in 1917, alienating United States sympathy and eventually drawing her in on the side of Britain and France, is too well known to need more than passing mention. Remembered less often after the war was the fact that of the forty British and Allied armoured fighting ships, including armoured cruisers, that the Germans and Turks destroyed, thirty-one were sent to the bottom either by the torpedo or the mine. Of fourteen British capital ships sunk by enemy action, only three succumbed to gunfire, all of these lightly armoured battle-cruisers.

Of the torpedo's two carriers, the submarine was by far the more damaging and influential, although the German Navy rarely had more than 100 of them at sea at any one time. Not only did the submarine sink some eleven million tons of merchant shipping, but was instrumental in bringing about the defensive state of mind that governed the activities of the British Grand Fleet from the very first days of the war. The torpedo's other carrier, the destroyer, also intervened decisively in the few big ships' surface actions causing even the boldest commanders to turn away from the enemy at the very moment when it seemed that a decision might be reached.

The underestimation of the power of the torpedo and its two carriers, the destroyer and submarine, by the world's great naval powers before and during the First World War must surely be classed as one of the most extraordinary miscalculations in the history of warfare. Instead of complex high speed manœuvrings, the operation of multitudinous technical equipment, leading to the grandeur of big-gun combat at sea, commanders-in-chief were mainly preoccupied with the risk of demoralisation of their men from idleness in harbour or anchorage, and the means to avoid discontent and even mutiny. By the spring of 1918 the British Grand Fleet was the subject of a carefully worked-out programme for filling time. A shop ship, "a veritable Army and Navy Stores" selling "everything from sports gear to caviare" toured from vessel to vessel doing excellent trade with men who had little other opportunity for spending their pay. Inter-ship boxing tournaments were popular. So were amateur dramatics. A store ship was converted into a floating theatre and moved from battleship to battleship, spending three days at each. The first day was spent in rehearsal and preparation of props. and scenery; the second day a performance was given to the ship's company; on the last evening selected officers and men from other ships were invited to the performance. Costumes and wigs were sent up by train from London and elaborate and spectacular lighting effects were produced by the ships' electricians. HMS *Warspite* won a high reputation by presenting a complete light opera based on Edward German's *Merrie England*, and Beatty's flagship even put on a Russian ballet to the music of Liszt.

It was no easy task to retain through the battle fleet both fighting efficiency and a sense of the importance of their rôle in relation to the distant Flanders fighting. Once every four weeks the fleet went to sea, screened by its flotillas, for evolutions and gun practice. On one of these occasions

King George V came north to reassure his sailors by his presence that they were not forgotten. Beatty took him out for a shoot, although he was "rather afraid of stopping out too long, as the enemy submarines are always about, and it would have been a tragedy if we had been torpedoed with him on board. . . ."[4]

But the British commander-in-chief never quite lost hope that the decisive meeting between the two great fleets would take place. "Please God our time will soon come when we can put (the fleet) to the test and reap our reward," he wrote to his wife in June 1918. Three months later the prospects of battle seemed as remote as ever. "It is terrible to think that after all these weary months of waiting we shall not have an opportunity of striking a blow." Only the danger of a desperate suicide stroke by the High Seas Fleet sustained Beatty during those last months of war and provided him with the means of keeping keen his crew's battle spirit. This "last coup," this "great blow with the High Seas Fleet," was still regarded by Beatty as a possible final expedient by the Kaiser even after the German Fleet had been fatally stricken by disaffection and mutiny. When the armistice terms were being drawn up, the danger seemed no less acute to Beatty, who was distinctly nettled when Marshal Foch recommended that the German Navy should be obliged to surrender only its submarines, as they alone had committed any damage. Beatty, of course, would have none of this, and on 21 November, 1918, the German High Seas Fleet and the British Grand Fleet met at last, for the first time since that single mist- and smoke-wreathed brief engagement off Jutland nearly three years earlier.

2 Around Chesapeake Bay

THE RESTRICTED RÔLE of the big gun during four and a half years of sea warfare did not destroy or even reduce its status. On the contrary, the principle of mounting the biggest guns on the biggest ships had never been so highly regarded as in 1919. In the new naval race, between Japan and the United States, which had begun long before the signing of the armistice in Europe, and which was already making Anglo-German naval competition at the beginning of the century look quite a tame business, the giant capital ship still remained unchallenged as the ultimate weapon. Neither torpedo, nor mine, nor aerial bomb had made apparent mark on the battle fleet's intended function and rôle in combat. By the end of 1918, heavy bombers were being completed that could have raided Berlin, and both the bomb load and the accuracy of bombardment had increased immeasurably. The use of the heavy bomber against the fleet was, however, scarcely contemplated. But it was machines like the Handley-Page and Martin bombers and the American NC-type flying boat that were soon to succeed the torpedo boat of the 1880s and the submarine of the first years of the century to form the spearhead of the new theoretical offensive against the big battleship.

This was a battle of words and science that was to make

the earlier controversies seem small affairs. It was to last some twenty years, marked by bitter rancour, endless debate, elaborate mock trials, committees of investigation, learned reports, and the ceaseless development of ever more formidable weapons of attack and defence on both sides. This twenty years' conflict was to involve the reputation of naval and air force officers and politicians, some of whom were unforgivably self-interested or bigoted, some so absurdly and single-mindedly partisan as to be in the lunatic fringe, but the great majority either sensibly far-sighted or at least honest in their endeavour to form a rational judgment. It is a sorry story, compounded of pathos, folly and both good and evil intentions; of remarkable application and misapplication of scientific development; of judgment and misjudgment both on the grandest scale.

It is a curious reflection on the service mind, and on human nature, that both in Britain and America the most influential and most publicised attacks on traditional battleship policy came from retired admirals who had during their active career done more than most of their contemporaries to strengthen the battle fleet and perpetuate the legend of the big gun. Among those on the Royal Navy's retired list who led the anti-battleship school were Admiral of the Fleet Lord Fisher of Kilverstone, and Admiral Sir Percy Scott, the great gunnery expert. In the United States, the stoutest naval campaigner for air power was Rear-Admiral Sims, who had commanded the American naval forces in European waters.

In the summer of 1913, one of the most outspoken and fiery officers in the Royal Navy had retired from the service at the age of sixty, with the rank of Admiral and a baronetcy. Admiral Sir Percy Scott was a bearded, tough little man who acted, and used violent language, in a manner that caused him to be marked as an eccentric, even in a service that was rich in colourful characters. In a popular phrase of the time, Percy Scott did not suffer fools gladly, nor did he much care for anyone who contradicted him about anything. He numbered only enemies or loyal admirers from past vendettas among his fellow officers. In 1900, at a time when "the importance of good gunnery was, in practice, still strangely and culpably neglected throughout the British Fleet" and the heavy shell was making only one hit in three under the absurdly easy prize-firing regulations of the day, Percy Scott created a sensation by scoring 76.92 per cent hits with the guns of his first-class cruiser *Terrible*. Five years later Fisher appointed Percy Scott to the new office of Inspector of Target Practice, defending his action against the attacks of Scott's many critics thus: "I don't care if he drinks, gambles, and womanises; *he hits the target*." When Percy Scott relinquished this post in 1907, the British Fleet's gunnery, according to Marder, was some two and a half times faster and more accurate than it had been ten years before; which says nothing at all for Victorian gunnery standards. When Percy Scott finally retired, full of honours, achievements and lingering animosities, he at once began attempting to bring about a revolution which, if successful, would signal the end of the big gun to which he had given his life. In a letter written in 1913 and reprinted in *The Times* on 5 June, 1914, he declared that "battleships are no use either for defensive or offensive purposes. Submarines and aeroplanes have entirely revolutionised naval warfare."

There was no defence against the submarine, he said, "they can only be attacked by airships dropping bombs on them. . . . What we need is an enormous fleet of submarines, airships and aeroplanes, and a few fast cruisers . . . naval officers will no longer live on the sea, but either above it or under it."

The astonishment and outrage which this full-column letter aroused two months before Britain began hostilities with Germany, equipped with a negligible submarine and air service and the greatest battle fleet the world had ever known, were considerable. But Percy Scott had to wait for nearly five years before renewing his campaign, the consequences of which will be examined later.

"I usually know what I want to say and I usually succeed in saying it," was the uncompromising testimony of a senior American naval officer speaking before a Senate Committee on naval policy in 1919. It was a declaration that might well have been adopted by all the protagonists in the opening rounds of the bomb versus battleship controversy that got under way within months of the ending of a war—in which neither weapon had played a very active part. This officer, who had a good deal to say both during and after his active service life, was William Sowden Sims of the United States Navy, the one American naval figure of any consequence to emerge from the First World War. William Sims was not one of the earliest disciples of air power. That remarkable officer, Bradley A. Fiske, for one, was advocating airborne torpedoes (and actually took out a patent for such a weapon), as early as 1912. Sims remained loyal to the big gun and the big ship for the full length of his active service career. He had been firmly on the side of the traditionalists when men like Alexander Graham Bell were writing in 1909 that "the airship will revolutionise warfare" and that "the nation that secures control of the air will ultimately control the world." In the following year Sims had written to a friend who had been asked to write an article on the power of the airship, "I am afraid that you are up against it good and hard . . . provided that you expect to show that such craft can ever be particularly dangerous to men-of-war. According to the papers, one of the Wright brothers has stated that it would be impracticable to hit anything by dropping a projectile from his flying machine. The Wright man is right, all right." Ten years later, in 1919, when he was appointed President of the War College, Sims's views appeared to be unchanged. Late in December, his attention had been drawn to a letter in *The Times* above the name of his old hero and friend, Percy Scott. Scott had returned to the fray against the capital ship with new gusto immediately after the end of the war, and in *The Times* of 12 December, 1919, in the course of a long attack on the administrative inefficiency of the Admiralty, he pronounced the aeroplane as "the most important arm of offence and defence. . . . If the surface battleship is dead," continued Scott, "then its death will greatly affect the future Navy. I said before the war that she was dead; I and a great many naval officers now think she is more than dead, if that is possible."

According to Sims's biographer, Sims had commented on this letter, "I should think that he would keep reasonably quiet. All the aeroplane-carrying ships in the world could

not make an attack upon a foreign country unless they were
supported by a battleship force that was superior to that
of the enemy."[5] But during the course of the next twelve
months Sims entirely repudiated this view. During 1920,
at the War College, Sims made much use of the Game
Board for the instruction of officers in naval tactics. In
one of the exercises two sides were given an equal sum of
money, one being instructed to spend their appropriation
only on aircraft carriers, the other on a mixed fleet. In
the "naval war" that was then played out on the board, it
was proved, at least to Sims's satisfaction, that a fleet of
twenty-two aircraft carriers could destroy an enemy
possessing sixteen battleships and six each aircraft carriers
and battle cruisers. No one can say how far the result of
these War Games, which were always open to almost any
interpretation, were the cause of Sims's change of heart,
but by January 1921, he was writing, "This afternoon we
had a discussion with the entire staff over the whole matter,
and it was easy to see that the question of the passing of the
battleship was not an agreeable one to various members."

Thus, within two years of the ending of the war, the
most vocal and distinguished retired gunnery officers in
both the United States and British navies were actively
campaigning for the end of the big gun that had brought
them honours and seniority in their service.

The weight of opinion of elderly admirals like Sims in
America and Scott and Fisher in Britain, played an important part in the struggle for supremacy between the
aeroplane and the battleship in the years 1921 to 1924.
But as in any revolt demanding endurance, imagination,
courage and cunning, the frontal attacks were led by the

younger combatants, in this case by the aviators themselves: by Goering in Germany, Douhet in Italy, in Britain by Air Marshal Sir Hugh Trenchard, and in America by General William Mitchell. These last two strongly contrasting men were fighting for similar but not identical ends, and used very different methods of attack. One succeeded magnificently, and the other failed disastrously. One died as the honoured and revered symbol of the service to which he had given his life, the very apotheosis of air power; the other died forgotten by most of his countrymen and remembered by a few as a faintly comic eccentric showman. The contests fought by both these men were marked by wrath and tragi-comedy; but the supreme irony was that when they both retired from the field of battle, one the victor and the other the vanquished, the big-gun battleship was still recognised in Britain and America as the backbone of the fleet.

William Lendrum Mitchell was only thirty-eight when he arrived in France to take part in his second war. He was just in time to witness General Nivelle's 1917 spring offensive, and saw at first hand the terrible price of a typical frontal assault offensive by infantry against a strongly entrenched enemy. Within nine days, from Nivelle's cry of *"L'heure est venue!"* on 16 April the French lost 187,000 men. The effect on the young American aviation colonel was profound. "The war is a slaughterhouse performance from beginning to end on the ground," he wrote. "Maybe one side makes a few yards or maybe a mile and thousands of men are killed. It is not a war, it is simply slaughter. War is getting at the vitals of the enemy, that is, to shoot him in the heart. This kind of war is like clipping off one finger, then a toe, then his nose and gradually eating into his vitals." Mitchell had flown over the front lines in a French plane, the first American airman to do so. After watching the "waves of 'horizon blue,' broken here and there by the khaki of colonial divisions, swarming forward into the mist and battle-smoke of that dull and overcast morning, carrying the hopes of a nation";[6] and then the overworked and inadequate medical services attempting to deal with the huge number of dead and wounded sprawled in the mud, it is not surprising that this eager and energetic American, already predisposed in favour of large-scale bombardment as a means of breaking the European *impasse*, should at once have become his country's leading proponent of air power.

For the second time within a generation, man had discovered the means to wage war in an entirely new element. While German submarines were actively engaged in the blockade of Britain and the destruction of her merchantmen in millions of tons, the heavy bombing machine was beginning to reveal a fresh dimension in the art of warfare. Raids by German heavy bombing aircraft —the Gothas that succeeded the slow and vulnerable Zeppelins—were causing alarm, despondency and severe loss of war production from absenteeism in Britain, even if they inflicted only slight damage. Command of the air was becoming an important factor in the land operations on the western front. But most important of all, a small core of opinion was growing among those associated with the new air arm who were beginning to discern a possible means of escape from the stalemate that had seized the

35

great armies and fleets from the first days of the war. From those few who could rise above it all into this intoxicating new element, to view the struggle below, to soar in a few minutes across the ravaged land, there developed a messiah-like spirit. It was born of a compound of military intellect and calculation and anger, and compassion for this hideous interminable waste of human life. It was impelled by a zeal that brooked no compromise. It arrived as a ready-made panacea, pat on time, tailored to the circumstances; and it had no more determined disciple than Brigadier-General William Mitchell.

From the town of Chalons close behind the front line, Mitchell wrote home long reports on all aspects of air operations on the western front, and in Chalons he experienced a German bombing attack. "I was using my small Corona typewriter by the light of two candles," he wrote in his diary. "As I wrote I heard the hum of a strange airplane motor and almost immediately—Zing! Zing! Zing! and all the doors and windows shook. . . . No one can ever tell me there is nothing in airplane bombing."[7] Even before he became aviation chief of the American First Army, with promotion to Brigadier-General, Mitchell had recognised that his mission in life would be first the conquest of Germany through the medium of air power, and then the creation of a defence force for his own country based on the aeroplane, with the two older services in only a subsidiary capacity. He set about the first with passionate energy, a disregard for procedure, an intolerance for the supposed shortcomings in others, an impatience accompanied by the use of the richest invective; all of which were soon to become familiar to the service chiefs in Washington, and later to the whole American nation.

Mitchell served with distinction and bravery during the few months when America possessed an Air Force of any significance in Europe. He fought well in the air, and, like Sims, he found that his struggles against incompetency and muddle across the Atlantic, and against his senior officers for greater recognition of his arm, were useful preparation for his future work. But he never learnt in France the value of restraint. "The General Staff is now trying to run the Air Service with just as much knowledge of it as a hog knows about ice skating," he wrote in his diary in April, 1916. "It is terrible to have to fight with an organisation of this kind instead of devoting all our energy to the powerful enemy on our front. I have had many talks with General Pershing . . . some of them very heated, with much pounding on the table on both sides. One time he told me that if I kept insisting that the organisation of the Air Service be changed he would send me home. I answered that if he did he would soon come after me . . ."[8] Neither officer came home until his time expired, Mitchell to an influential desk job in Washington, buoyed up by the strength of his ardent convictions, and utterly confident that he would see them established.

For the victorious great powers, 1919 was a year of momentous defence reappraisal, brought about at once by the need to cut back military force to normal peace-time strength, and in America, by the need to meet the new dangers already rising in the East. Those who remained to command were left stripped of many of the great responsibilities they had become accustomed to bearing.

For men like William Mitchell, a professional soldier since boyhood and a man of action, the contrast between leading a massive air force into battle in Europe and the debilitating atmosphere of politics in Washington, must have been hard to bear. The jockeying for power and influence and appropriations was in full swing, and the scent of fear for lost status was heavy in the air of the capital, when Mitchell took over office on 1 March, 1919, as assistant to the new chief of the Air Service, General Menoher. He had accepted the appointment less "to settle accounts for the colossal waste and incompetence of the swivel-chair administrators of the aviation programme"[8] than to strike the first blows in the battle for an independent air force. To justify a new service to a nation that had never shown much interest in expensive armed forces in times of peace, it would be necessary to cut deeply into the influence of the two older arms. Although he could not claim any special knowledge of maritime war, Mitchell recognised that the navy was the most vulnerable target. The United States Navy, it could be argued, had done nothing of distinction and importance since the massacres of the Spanish-American War; it was highly expensive in men and money; and its whole *raison d'être* was invested in the battleship, a weapon that was being claimed, by certain British admirals who should have known, as an obsolete weapon. Mitchell, and those officers close to him who had fought with him in France and were to remain as loyal allies to the end, came to the decision that the navy should be their first target.

The contest would have been brief and decisive if the politically naïve Mitchell, and his straight-talking, hard-hitting henchmen, had not had allies. But other powerful figures, for various motives, were prepared to give the weight of their authority to the cause. There were the aircraft manufacturers, for example, a body of young, vigorous industrialists. Many of the army generals back from France were prepared to testify that the bombing plane was now such an important weapon of destruction that at least the air arm justified an independent service. Even before William Sims threw in his lot in favour of the abolition of the capital ship, other senior naval officers, including the historian and thinker, Admiral W. F. Fullam, were prepared to make public their view that "sea power, or fighting power, in the future will be largely dependent upon control of the air." But through all the committees and sub-committees of investigation, the courts of inquiry and boards and missions of study, through all the political manœuvrings and the stormy ebb and flow of the tides of influence that continued for some five years and involved many public figures, the focus of attention remained on William Mitchell, the indomitable and tireless publicist.

Only five weeks after his Washington appointment, Mitchell had been invited to a meeting of the General Board of the Navy Department to discuss the future of naval aviation policy. There was already talk in the Navy Department of a series of trials to test the effect of aerial bombs against warships. Mitchell, at once recognising these trials in simpler terms as a means to show the world how a bomb could sink a battleship, seized the idea and adopted it as his own. "We can try a good many things out around Chesapeake Bay," he is supposed to have told the Board. It was "a very nice and interesting meeting," Mitchell recalled two years later when his relations with the navy were less cordial. The navy remained non-committal, while agreeing that there were many joint problems to solve. Some eighteen months later, tests were carried out on the old battleship *Indiana* by placing fixed charges representing aerial bombs on her deck, and by carrying out dummy bomb attacks from flying boats. It was not until the *Illustrated London News* published startling pictures, acquired from some unspecified source, of the devastating results of these trials, that the public heard anything about them. The official navy reports, prepared by the Director of Naval Gunnery, and made public to appease public curiosity, stated that, "The entire experiment pointed to the improbability of a modern battleship being either destroyed or completely put out of action by aerial bombs." But because of the secrecy under which the trials had been held and because they had coincided with the Presidential elections and therefore inevitably aroused political passions, the affair was investigated by the House Committee on Naval Affairs. The appearance of Admiral Sims as a new recruit to the air power school alone made certain that Mitchell would, after all, have his way, and that future trials would be a public exhibition of the power of the bomber "around Chesapeake Bay."

The bombing in 1921 of the surrendered German battleship *Ostfriesland* and other warships off Chesapeake Bay, could never have aroused such wide national interest and taken on the guise of a great baseball game or contest for a boxing title but for the matchless publicity sense of William Mitchell. He had already many times exhibited an appreciation of the value of the spectacle and the creation of a picture of air power to match those firmly established images that had grown round the two older services. While in France, he had cultivated the figure of himself as a swashbuckling knight of the air, fearless and daring as a pilot, speeding from airfield to airfield in a vast racing car and dressed flashily in unorthodox uniform. Between bombing raids on the enemy he devised a new form of propaganda warfare aimed at his own army. Mitchell was the inventor of the leaflet raid. "DOUGHBOYS!" was the headline to one of these leaflets. "While you are giving the Boche hell on the ground, we are helping you to the limit in the air. . . . Do not think we are not on the job if you cannot see us. Most of our planes work so far to the front that they cannot be seen from the lines. Some of the enemy planes may break through our airplane barrage in front of you, and may sometimes bomb and machine-gun you, but in the last month we have dropped ten tons of bombs for every one the Boche has dropped. For every Boche plane you see over you, the Boche sees ten allied planes over him. . . . After reading this pass it on to your buddies." Back home in America, Mitchell was always in the news as a result of some outspoken article he had written, and he strove to keep the image of air power before the public by organising flying displays and record-breaking flights all over the country.

By early 1921 the ground had been well prepared for Mitchell's plan to show how bombs could sink ships. His claim for funds for the air service before the House Appropriations Committee offered him the moment to hurl down his challenge with the certainty of being widely reported. "All we want to do is to have you gentlemen

watch us attack a battleship . . . All we want is a chance
to demonstrate these things and have you gentlemen see
them . . . Give us the warships to attack, and come and
watch it . . . If you want a demonstration of the effect
of bombardment against a naval vessel, we are prepared to
give you that demonstration now." Secretary of the Navy
Josephus Daniels, no mean publicist himself and by then the
confirmed foe of Mitchell, retorted that the bomber would
never be a menace to the armoured battleship, and that he
would "gladly stand bareheaded on the deck or at the wheel
of any battleship while Mitchell tries to take a crack at me
from the air . . ."; a duel that would, according to the Balti-
more *Sun*, "thrill many a heart to witness." From the
moment when five ex-German warships arrived in America
for experimental purposes, on the understanding that they
would be destroyed within six months, there was no further
doubt that Mitchell would at last get his wish, although
it was not thought suitable that the Secretary of the Navy
should offer himself as a personal target.

Mitchell prepared for the tests as if they were a military
operation, training to perfection his picked bombing
crews, arranging to have built special bombs of up to 2000
lb., by far the largest in the world, and a gyroscopic bomb
sight of a special kind. The trials began on 21 June, 1921,
and took place at a distance of about one hundred miles
from the nearest shore, in itself a handicap for the short
range bombers of that time, and were as elaborate as a
modern nuclear weapons test. A train of eight battleships,
cruisers, destroyers, hospital ships, tenders and other small
craft stood by. "If the series had been prepared by a master
impresario, it could not have turned out better theatre or

provided greater suspense to the audience. In supreme charge was the Commander-in-Chief of the Atlantic Fleet, Admiral Henry B. Wilson. The master of ceremonies was Captain A. W. Johnson . . . operating from the control ship, the *Shawmut*, which carried the official board of observers. But the star of the performance was the guest-artist from the army, General William Mitchell."[7] The main audience was accommodated on board the naval transport *Henderson*, and consisted of high officials of both services, congressmen, diplomats and naval attachés and correspondents. Overhead there hovered naval airships, and photographic planes swooped low in readiness to witness the onslaught. It was a misty dawn and the intended victim of Mitchell's bombs lay low and grey in the sluggish swell, the centre of attention for all those in the great concourse of vessels. She was the preliminary "warming up" target, the big ocean-going German submarine U-117.

It was still faintly misty when the sound of the first planes was heard. Three of them in formation came into sight, split up, and dived down in turn, levelling out to drop their bombs from a height of 1,100 feet. Two salvoes sufficed to send the U-boat to the bottom. A destroyer and the light cruiser *Frankfurt* went the same way in succeeding trials. Mitchell, who led some of the attacks himself and observed them all from the air, was jubilant. The standard of accuracy of the army bombardiers was excellent, especially when seen in comparison with the naval aircraft which scored only two hits out of eighty on the radio-controlled target battleship *Iowa* in another exercise. Mitchell felt that he had already gone a long way towards proving the vulnerability of surface ships to air power, but most observers held their judgment until the real test against the heavily armoured and modern battleship *Ostfriesland*. Mitchell himself knew that final success or failure depended on the accuracy of his bomb-aimers and the effectiveness of his hastily-built giant bombs against this dreadnought. "Looking down on her, she appeared like a bulldog where the *Frankfurt* had looked like a swan," wrote Mitchell, who had already spent many anxious hours flying off Chesapeake Bay with his observer in his little reconnaissance plane. "She was sullen and dark and we knew we had a tough old nut to crack. . . . We had already proved that we could sink any other ship except a battleship . . . Still all this would be forgotten if we failed to kill, bury and to cover up the *Ostfriesland*."[8] In the event of the expected failure of the bombers, orders had already been given by the navy for the new battleship *Pennsylvania* to destroy the dreadnought with her 14-inch guns at spectacularly long range.

The morning of 20 July was dour and disagreeable, with low clouds, a swirling sea mist, a twenty-five knot breeze, and a heavy swell that caused discomfort to the army and civilian observers. The exercise began with a series of attacks by both army and navy machines carrying progressively heavier bombs, each attack being followed by a careful examination of the damage caused. Six direct hits were made during the first phase, but almost fifty per cent of the bombs proved to be duds and the damage caused by the others was superficial. The medium weight bombs of around six hundred pounds dropped from 1500 feet in the afternoon tore holes in the *Ostfriesland's* upper deck, and by four o'clock she was listing astern. Still the examining officers who came aboard could find no evidence of mortal damage or even of her inability to steam back to base had she been in real combat.

In all fifty-two bombs had been dropped, and the *Ostfriesland* was still afloat. Although Mitchell's biggest bombs had not been used that day, naval observers regarded the result as a sufficient triumph to justify the immediate dispatch of a fast destroyer carrying reporters back to land to telephone their stories and break the news that the battleship had won. The following morning, with newspapers all over the country carrying headlines proclaiming his alleged failure, Mitchell carried out an inspection of his sixteen crack bombers, half loaded up with thousand-pounders, the others carrying the experimental "tonners," and once more carefully briefed the pilots on the importance of this last opportunity.

Soon after 8 am the first of the bombers sighted the *Ostfriesland*. The battered and dirty dreadnought was lying stationary and helpless, the bull's eye within the target ring of the United States Atlantic Fleet steaming in a circle two miles from her. At 8.23 the first bomber went in, levelling off at 2000 feet and dropping a thousand-pounder direct on to the forecastle. Four more planes followed, scoring two more hits in such rapid succession that the signal from the *Shawmut* ordering a cease-fire, demanded by the rules after a hit, was not observed. A confusion of signals then followed, beginning a dispute between Mitchell and the navy umpires which was later to grow into an acrimonious and widely-reported investigation. The remaining bombers were ordered back to their base, and in a fit of frustration and pique the pilots swooped low down over the fleet with their remaining live bombs and dropped them in a highly intimidating pattern within half a mile of the warships, before disappearing towards Langley Field. After this frightening experience, the navy observers hastened once again to the *Ostfriesland*. In a short time they were jubilantly signalling that still the battleship's wounds were not mortal. The protective deck of the battleship designed to withstand the plunging fire of long-range heavy ordnance, had not been pierced. It now seemed clear to everyone present that the guns of the *Pennsylvania* would have to be called in to finish off the *Ostfriesland* during the afternoon. But the last of Mitchell's bombers were already on their way from Langley Field, accompanied by Mitchell who flew ahead and five hundred feet above them like a trainer leading a contingent of heavyweight pugilists into the ring. When they were over the *Pennsylvania* Mitchell swung aside, and in a carefully rehearsed evolution of defiance, the bombers formed up into line astern formation and flew slowly past their commander as if being reviewed. Then the first bomber peeled off and headed for the target ship.

The first giant bomb went down at 12.18. "It blazed in the sunshine as it tumbled over and over in its course, landing on the crest of a wave one hundred feet off the starboard bow of the warship," wrote the *New York Herald's* reporter. "There was a muffled roar and a great splash of water, which let out black and white smoke." Again disregarding the rules, which were intended to allow the observers to examine the progressive damage caused by successive bombs, Mitchell sent in his bombers one after

46

the other, determined to finish off the battleship. Five more "tonners" followed the first down within the next few minutes, allowing only brief glimpses of the battleship between the subsiding of one great water spout and the black cloud and erupting of the next. The last bomber stood by, waiting to give the *coup de grâce*; but as the last of the smoke and spray cleared the *Ostfriesland*, it could be seen that it would not be needed. The battleship was listing heavily to starboard and her bows were high out of the water, revealing a great gash in her rusty hull. By 12.36 the battleship's stern was awash and she continued to sink deeper and deeper until she was standing almost vertically on her end in the stained water. She looked, at this moment, like the memorial stone to all the battleships in the world. Twenty-one minutes after the first bomb had fallen alongside her, the battleship had gone, and the last bomber flew low over the confusion of bubbles and loose wreckage to drop its bomb in a cruel gesture of exultation.

"A bomb was fired to-day that will be heard around the world," was the comment of the army's chief of ordnance, General Williams. This was perhaps the only unarguable conclusion on the most important weapons trial ever conducted up to that time.

Neither to Billy Mitchell swooping victoriously over the observation ship *Henderson*, nor to those who responded to his arm-waving from the cockpit, could there have seemed any doubt that the great dispute had been settled. From now on, surely the striking and defensive power of the world's fleets would be invested in the bomber instead of the battleship. But hardly had he landed back at Langley Field, than the totally conflicting interpretations of the trials were being spread publicly and in the Washington service departments. That this was news, nobody attempted to deny. But that the destruction of one armoured vessel signified the end of the big gun and its platform, which had ruled the seas for centuries, was hardly likely to be accepted either by navalists (Marder's convenient coined term), by a public that had for so long invested their image of sea power in the capital ship, or by the powerful industrial groups from gunmakers to shipbuilders and steel manufacturers, who had for so long lived by the warship. Of course the arguments could be weighted either way. The bombs were new and undeveloped, claimed the Mitchell supporters, or one would have sufficed. A thousand heavy bombers could have been built and used for the attack, for the price of a single battleship—which took four years to build and was usually obsolete before it was finished. The bombers were designed for a war that was already fading into history; imagine the state of the bomber—twice as fast with twice the load and with precision bombsights—by the next war!

But this was no fair test, argued the navalists. The *Ostfriesland* was stationary, a sitting target, with no helmsman to take evasive action, no crew to fight back with guns and repair the damage. She had no defensive fighter planes, and she was an obsolete old wreck anyway. The renegade theorist, Admiral Fullam, came back with the argument that "there is nothing so difficult to sink as a naval hulk. A naval vessel with its boilers, engines and steering gear in operation, and with its magazines filled, its guns in use, with torpedoes in place, depth charges in

48

position, and gun crews at their stations, will be far more easily destroyed than a hulk lying dead in the water with no explosives aboard. Why, anybody can know that."

For weeks after the *Ostfriesland* went down, the lessons of her destruction were debated up and down the country by interested and disinterested parties, shrilly and soberly. The most conservative navalists claimed that the exercise proved nothing; the British naval attaché in Washington stated that the serious nature of the exercise was being played down and that "the effects of 2000 lb. bombs bursting alongside the *Ostfriesland* and of a 1000 lb. bomb on the *Frankfurt*, were so immediate and overwhelming as to render it immaterial whether those vessels were possessed of watertight integrity or not." Mitchell, who had learnt the value of repetition, simply claimed over and over again that the battleship was finished.

But slowly, inevitably, the mantle of considered compromise descended on the battlefield. Not all the soothing voices were wise in their moderation, but some arrived at an interpretation that stood the test of time, at least until the tempo reached a pitch few could be expected to follow. The armoured battleship had met numerous threats in the past, from the submarine, the torpedo boat, the mine; and had adapted itself and survived. At some future date it might be forced to relinquish supremacy to the aircraft. Franklin Delano Roosevelt, as Assistant Secretary of the Navy, had already admitted (12 September, 1919 in the Senate Sub-committee on Military Affairs) "that later on in the future, aviation may make surface ships practically impossible to be used as an arm"; and in Britain the tentative preparations were being made for that time. But, as an editorial in the *Scientific American* of 6 August, 1921, put it, "the dramatic sinking of the *Ostfriesland* . . . does not prove that the day of the big battleship is passed. . . . The one outstanding lesson is this—that since aerial bombs can work much deadly havoc on a dreadnought it is imperative that a fleet be provided with every known defensive means of driving off or destroying the enemy bombing machine." In the same magazine Commander E. G. Allen put the case of the United States Navy with sensible clarity, claiming that given careful watertight sub-division, adequate armour in the right places, sufficient anti-aircraft gun protection and "protective pursuit planes" the battleship would survive any air attack in the foreseeable future. "Notwithstanding all the hysteria concerning the passing of the capital ship as a type, it must be remembered that the cheapest and most powerful unit weapon is the gun." From Germany even the defeated Admiral Scheer, who knew better than most commanders-in-chief what it was like to be locked in harbour, gave his comments. "Even though the factor of defence did not enter into these experiments, it cannot be denied that the prospects are favourable to the aeroplane —since an attacking fleet cannot remain in motion permanently," he said. "It requires rest for the engines, time for taking on board munitions, fuel and oil supplies, it must dock for repairs and lie at anchor—and it is then that the opportunity for an attack presents itself."

Finally, on 20 August, the official report on the *Ostfriesland* trials by the army and navy board was published. It recognised that while aircraft were certainly capable of sinking battleships, or "any naval vessels at present constructed . . . the battleship is still the backbone of the fleet and the bulwark of the nation's sea defence." It was an uncompromising document, signed by Mitchell's old antagonist from the war, and the most respected military figure in America, General Pershing. Mitchell was appalled when he read it, considering it as criminally partial, an outrage, a crime against the nation and a personal affront. He submitted his resignation at once, hastily withdrew it, and set about a new campaign that would end in personal catastrophe.

To Mitchell the demise of the battleship and the future omnipotence of the bomber were such simple, clear-cut military facts that further debate was futile. Such was his impatience, and his lack of appreciation of the naval mind's preoccupation with theory, that he made the elementary mistake of using the apparent vulnerability to bombs of target ships as the principal demonstration of his beliefs. As a born showman he suffered under the delusion that a total reappraisal of defence policy would come about because he was able to prove, by a single, highly-publicised spectacle, the vulnerability of one steel-cased man-of-war to airborne high-explosive.

3 *Kilkenny Cats*

Wɪᴛʜɪɴ ᴀ ꜰᴇᴡ ᴡᴇᴇᴋꜱ of his arrival on the Western Front in April 1917, William Mitchell included a call on General Hugh Trenchard, then commanding the Royal Flying Corps in France, in his eager fact-finding tour on behalf of American aviation. Trenchard was already a feared and formidable figure, "very tall, very broad-shouldered, with shaggy eyebrows and a deep voice that had fittingly given him the name of 'Boom',"[9] according to the man who was later to serve close to him for so many years as Secretary of State for Air. Mitchell himself found Trenchard "decided in manner and direct in speech," but appears to have been dismayed neither by his piercing deep-set eyes, his rank, his manner, nor his reputation. The American major told the British general that he had come to find out what made the Flying Corps tick—how it was organised, what equipment it used, how it was supplied, how it fought; and adding parenthetically that he would like to join in some operations.

This was a fairly big order, Trenchard replied, and asked him whether it was Mitchell's idea that he had nothing else to do and "how long he was prepared to wait for an answer." Mitchell told him that, with the excellent British organisation, a day and a half would doubtless suffice.

Mitchell later wrote in his diary that Trenchard's judgment "inspired my immediate confidence," and his subsequent tour of inspection of Trenchard's headquarters and RFC flying fields made a profound impression on him. Here was the translation into reality of his own dream of air power. While Trenchard was proud of his force, and a brilliant commander of it, he still regarded it at this time only as a corps, as a spotting, reconnaissance and bombing support group to the Army. It was the brash American major who, in 1917, already recognised in the RFC an entirely new arm that would revolutionise military philosophy and destroy the traditional rôles of the older services.

The sacred principle of the indivisibility of the air and the paramountcy of air power was a lesson Trenchard was to learn long after it had been acquired by Mitchell. But what Mitchell could never learn from Trenchard was his political wisdom, doggedness, his aptitude for attracting wise allies to his cause, and the comparative sophistication of his qualities as a fighter. "He's a man after my own heart," Trenchard said later of Mitchell. "If only he can break his habit of trying to convert opponents by killing them, he'll go far."[10] When they were both furiously engaged in battle with their respective navies, and Trenchard was observing from afar and with anxiety the *Ostfriesland* trials, he regretted that he had not sought to revive their old wartime friendship. When "Mitchell, the showman, seemed to be at greater odds than ever with Mitchell the air prophet," Trenchard felt he might still have been able to persuade the American to temper his extremism in order to better his chances of achieving his aims.

It is a good deal simpler to see why Mitchell failed in his

53

mission in America than it is to recognise the reason for Hugh Trenchard's totally unexpected success in retaining an independent air arm in Great Britain. Trenchard, who had done so much to build up the Royal Flying Corps as an auxiliary to the British armies in France, opposed the formation of the RAF in 1918 as a separate service, resigned as first Chief of Air Staff two weeks after a conflict of opinion with Lord Rothermere, the first Secretary of State for Air, and yet survived the post-war upheaval to achieve fame as "the father of the RAF." If the RAF, for many years the only major independent air arm in the world, can be said to have a father, it is the people of London. In 1917 they had at least as high a regard for the power of the aeroplane as that possessed by the man who was to give ten years of his life to the preservation of his service. The Zeppelin and Gotha bombing raids on London and other cities were on a small scale, and the fear they aroused seems strange to us to-day. Mixed with the fear was indignation and wounded pride at the way in which, for example, German aircraft sailed slowly over London in broad daylight, dropping their bombs at will and without opposition from either guns or fighters. Urgent steps were demanded of the politicians, and on 11 July, 1917 the Cabinet set up a committee on Air Organisation and Home Defence. Just five weeks later Lieutenant-General Jan Smuts, that wise and venerable prophet, placed before the War Cabinet his proposals to form a separate air force. "The day may not be far off," ran one passage of the Smuts Committee report, "when aerial operations with their devastation of enemy lands and destruction of industrial and populace centres on a vast scale, may become the principal operations of war, to which the older forms of military and naval operations may become secondary and subordinate." It was the first official pronouncement to accept the enormous potential power of this new war arm, and it came at a time of near-despair when schemes of all kinds were hurried through in an attempt to break the deadlock on the Western Front. In peace time it might have taken ten years of committee work, debate and counter-debate to produce anything so controversial and fundamental as a third force. But the Air Ministry was created within weeks, simply by an Order in Council on 3 January, 1918, and took over the duties of the old Air Board on 1 April, "a suitable charade for All Fools' Day," as Trenchard's biographer interprets his view of it. The birth of this third fighting force had been a painless one, and it was not until Trenchard was recalled as Chief of Air Staff after the end of the war that there grew in him the full passion of parental pride in the child he had weaned in Flanders, and which had now developed into lusty maturity.

Already in January, 1919, the RAF desperately needed strong paternal support. Now that its long-term implications became clear to the older service departments, the fight for the influence and the recognition of air power in Britain was to be as fierce and bitter as in the United States. All three services were suddenly faced with the imminent threat of economies, of public apathy and even hostility. Not only was a wave of pacifism sweeping over the nation, but Britain's debts were prodigious, many of her foreign assets had been sacrificed, and her vast productive machinery by which she lived had been dislocated in the cause of war. The service departments recognised with weary resignation, even before the fall of the Geddes Axe, that they were back to the old days. It was a question of the survival of the fittest, and survival depended on seeming to give value for money.

When he was recalled as Chief of Air Staff in 1919, Trenchard saw that his only chance of justifying the continued separate existence of a third force in the lean years that lay ahead was by proving that the RAF could accomplish more cheaply and more effectively certain tasks previously carried out by the army and the navy. To do this demanded shrewdness, a wide knowledge of military and naval history as well as of politics, and a flexibility of mind for manœuvre combined with singleness of purpose. Trenchard knew his opposition, respected its strength, recognised its weaknesses, and above all was blessed with brilliant allies steeped in the intricacies of ministerial manipulation, notably Samuel Hoare and Winston Churchill. Churchill, as Secretary of State for Air, and Trenchard, as Chief of Air Staff, made a formidable combination during the crucial first years of peace when demobilisation had developed into a mania for economy. When Churchill left the Air Ministry on 14 February, 1921 to become Secretary of State for the Colonies, he inherited a nationalistic crisis in Iraq which was involving the army in intolerably high expenditure. Trenchard had already convinced Churchill that the RAF could control this vast, disturbed area by a few squadrons of fighters and bombers, as a threat and occasional means of reprisal, at a fraction of the army's expenditure. By the end of the year, a policy of "control without occupation" by the RAF had been put into effect in the Middle East at the joint instigation of Trenchard and Churchill.

This astute piece of justification for the third force was carried out with smooth efficiency, and provided Trenchard with a powerful weapon in the far more formidable contest with the senior service which he knew lay ahead. Both in America and Britain, the early disputes between the air service and the army were more muted than the struggles with the navy. In fact, many of Mitchell's strongest supporters were "ground" generals who had seen the benefits the new arm could provide in the way of spotting, reconnaissance and long-range artillery through the bomber and even his quarrel with Pershing had originated from a conflict of personalities rather than of principles. Earl Haig, the C in C of the British Army in France, had remained on the most cordial terms with Trenchard, and the two men had co-operated wonderfully well in Flanders. There was never any question of the RAF seriously depriving the army of its fundamental functions, although there was some passing anxiety in the British War Office at the success of Trenchard's "control without occupation." The navy's situation in Britain, as in America, was much more vulnerable; and, bereft of the obscurities of committee reports, theoretical treatises and the niceties of inter-service exchanges, the controversy narrowed down once again to the ability of the battleship to resist its foes: the big-gun platform to survive the onslaught of other weapons than the big gun.

The polemics opened within months of the end of the war with the cry of "Sack the lot!" from an embittered old admiral, subsided for a short time while the professional contestants drew up their forces, and reached a climax during 1922 and 1923, after the *Ostfriesland's* sinking across the Atlantic.

In this brief story of the perilous life of the armoured battleship, it is neither easy nor just to make only passing reference to a figure of such stature and accomplishment as Admiral of the Fleet Lord Fisher of Kilverstone. Fisher's attitude to the submarine has already been mentioned. But his career had also taken in every convulsion endured by the battleship: its reluctant transition from sail to steam, from coal to oil, its defiance of the torpedo boat, its acceptance and relinquishment of the giant gun, and its constructional compromises that exploded at last into the *Dreadnought* of 1906. On the multitude of controversies in which the battleship was involved, until his death in 1920, Fisher was never lacking an opinion. His influence was already powerful in the 1880s, and during his two periods as First Sea Lord, 1904-10 and 1914-15, it was totally dominating. As he never failed to point out when opportunity arose, both during his period of power and after his "casting into the wilderness" following his dispute with Churchill in 1915, Fisher had opposed the admiralty's retention of sail, and fought for the water-tube boiler and the turbine, for homogeneity in the battle fleet, for greater attention to the threat of the mine as well as the submarine's torpedo, and was the chief inspiration behind the *Dreadnought* herself. The range of his mind was awe-inspiring; as a naval visionary he has never been surpassed. We have already seen that, before the first British boat had joined the fleet, he calculated that submarines would transform sea warfare.

Among his other more remarkable prophecies was the correct month and year of the opening of hostilities and of Asquith's departure from office as Prime Minister, both some five years before they occurred. Only Fisher before the war believed that the Germans would ever resort to unrestricted submarine warfare, only Fisher forecast in early 1915 that the battle fleet (every vessel of which had been conceived while he was in office) would not be needed, and that the war would last at least four years. And only Percy Scott from retirement and Fisher already seventy-three years old, were able in 1914 to visualise the fundamental impact air power would make on the fleet. While the more intelligent naval officers were recognising that airships and seaplanes might have their use for scouting purposes under suitable conditions, Fisher was showing real alarm at the ability of Zeppelins to carry, and drop on battleships, bomb loads of one ton. Seaplanes were still being used in the Royal Navy for reconnaissance purposes in the Second World War; but Fisher, who saw at once their drawbacks, was advising Jellicoe in April 1915 that "you *must* have aeroplanes! *Seaplanes no use.*"[3] After his downfall in May 1915, Fisher never regained power, and he became increasingly melancholy as he watched what he believed to be the mismanagement of the war by his successors at the Admiralty, by most of the soldiers, and by all the politicians of any importance. The fertility of his mind never diminished, and within three weeks of his death, he was still writing his staccato exclamatory letters to his old friend H. Wickham Stead at *The Times*. As if impelled by a last frenzy, his campaign against the battle fleet, to which he had dedicated his life, made even the outpourings of the vituperative Percy Scott* seem mild. Time and again he wrote of the battleship, and of the wasteful administrators who perpetuated them: "*Sack the lot!*" "Reiteration is the secret of conviction! Repetition is the soul of journalism! Advertisement is both! It's the soul of business! Keep on saying '*Sack the lot!*' and we shall be rid of them!" he concluded one of his letters to *The Times*. But serious reasoning was evident, too, for all the verbal violence in his memoirs and correspondence. "To build battleships merely to fight enemy battleships, so long as cheaper craft can destroy them, and prevent them of themselves protecting sea operations, is merely to breed Kilkenny cats unable to catch rats or mice," he wrote in *Records* (1919), and in two successive letters to *The Times* in the autumn of the same year: "It's as clear as daylight that future war at sea absolutely precludes the use of any vessel of war that can't go underwater, because aircraft will compel it. So why keep any of the present lot? . . . All you want is the present naval side of the air force!—that's the future navy . . . By land and sea the approaching prodigious aircraft development knocks out the present fleet, makes invasion practicable, cancels our country being an island, and transforms the atmosphere into the battleground of the future. . . ."

But by 1919 Fisher was popularly discredited. He had been shabbily treated. The King, who always disliked and suspected Fisher, omitted reference to him in his formal peace speech of thanks, and he was not invited to the

* 'Criminal, woeful, wicked, wanton, wilful waste,' Scott described battleships in *The Times*, March 24 1922. 'Twaddle,' and 'cock-and-bull' were two more of his favourite expressions.

surrender of the German fleet. There were still some men
of influence who believed in him, but they made up a small
minority, and it is unlikely that Beatty was seriously
disturbed by the intelligence in Fisher's letter of con-
gratulation on his appointment as First Sea Lord, that "the
whole aspect of sea war is so utterly changed by the
prodigious and daily development of aircraft."[3] If Beatty
could at that time have imagined the extent and bitterness
of the struggle that lay ahead of him, he might have
listened more carefully to his old First Sea Lord.

David Beatty's greatness and reputation, like the men-of-
war that he served in and personified, lay in his successful
fulfilment of the image expected of him. It is impossible
to imagine Beatty embracing any other rôle in sea warfare
than that of Commander-in-Chief, standing on the bridge
of his flagship as he leads a squadron of great ships in
pursuit of the enemy. When Fisher conceived his dreadnoughts, he did not produce for the Royal Navy only the
most advanced and formidable battleships in the world;
he also brought into being, for the comfort of the British
people, a new image of maritime power, with the human
element manifested in the steadfast figure of John Jellicoe.
Collectively, the dreadnought battle fleet and the men who
commanded it in 1914, gave Britain her twentieth-century
equivalent of "the wooden walls," and the sense of solidity
and security the people demanded. When Fisher's *Invincible*
was completed in March 1908, this first battle cruiser and
its successors in the Battle Cruiser Squadron similarly
demanded human personification that could satisfy the
image of swift, relentless attack for which these romantic

vessels were intended. David Beatty filled the rôle of dashing and gallant aggressor even more suitably than did Jellicoe as the dour defender. Everything was in his favour, and he could not have failed to become a national hero.

Queen Victoria once described young Beatty as "a nice-mannered boy." Certainly his charm, good looks, breeding, intelligence and highly developed sense of vocation made his success in the rapidly growing Royal Navy of the late Victorian and Edwardian years a certainty. The means to achieve greatness were placed neatly to hand and he grasped them and drew himself dexterously up the promotional ladder at a speed unmatched for a hundred years. At twenty-seven he was a commander, at twenty-nine a captain, when the average age was forty-two, at thirty-eight a flag-officer—by Special Order in Council. He took one grave risk in marrying a divorced woman, but his aplomb and self-confidence got him through, and she was the daughter of the millionaire, Marshall Field. For more than two years of war in the *Lion*, he commanded the battle cruisers, leading them as a reconnaissance and striking force on the occasions when the German fleet made known its presence. He scored an early and heartening success at the Battle of Heligoland Bight, and he never flinched from pressing home the attack, whatever might be the circumstances. It took uncommon courage at Jutland, for example, to persist in his engagement, with first Hipper and then Scheer, when his battle cruisers were unaccountably blowing up around him and his shell-fire appeared to be making little impression on the enemy.

Inevitably by the end of the war, when he accepted the

surrender of the German High Seas Fleet amid the idolatrous cheers of his own men, he had become something of an enlargement of his own public figure: his cap just that more angled, his hair a shade longer than ever, his handsome face even more bronzed, windswept and lined with anxiety that might, to the uncharitable, have seemed justified. At forty-eight he was an Admiral of the Fleet, an Earl, First Sea Lord, the most unsullied hero of the war. He was "Beatty of the Battle Cruisers"; although for the last two years of inaction he had commanded the Grand Fleet itself when Jellicoe was sent to the Admiralty to attempt to deal with the submarine menace. When, in 1920, the first hints of the struggle with the Air Ministry were discernible, David Beatty naturally became anxious about the status of the service he commanded. Not only was the greatest fleet the world had known being paid off and scrapped, and the building of new tonnage to replace the Jutland losses cancelled, but the third force, the new and upstart RAF, was threatening certain traditional naval responsibilities, and was even proposing to keep under its control the navy's flying branch.

The first brush occurred in 1921 when the Board of Admiralty became alarmed at the extent of Japanese and American naval rearmament. In spite of the critical state of the country's economy, Beatty demanded four new battle cruisers, each of almost double the displacement of his old *Lion*, with a speed of thirty-two knots and with an armament of nine 16-inch guns; the largest and most powerful warships designed, before or since, in Britain. He expected his request to be met with Treasury dismay and indignation, and he knew that approval could be interpreted only as a heavy blow against Trenchard and the RAF, then struggling manfully for public recognition. For weeks the old arguments raged. Navalists and airmen and their supporting politicians and suppliers bandied about the old dogmas and statistics: France was keeping a huge air force and was not giving a thought to battleships, so many thousands of bombers could be built for the price of these mastodons. "The big ship is absolutely essential," claimed the First Lord. "The bomb is one thousand times less efficient than the gun," claimed Admiral Sir Reginald Bacon. As was to happen so often in both Britain and America during the two decades between the wars, resort was made to a committee, under Arthur Bonar Law, who was to become Conservative Prime Minister in 1922. In March 1921, the committee came down emphatically in favour of Beatty's four giants, and orders were placed with shipyards soon afterwards.

Undaunted by this blow, Trenchard and his staff produced at the same time a memorandum attacking the construction of battleships, and somewhat contradictorily, aircraft carriers as well. The Air Ministry's case was that the carrier was as expensive as a battleship and even more vulnerable, and that shore-based aircraft would be much more effective in times of war for protecting "The Imperial Lifeline." On the age-old principle that attack is the best form of defence, Trenchard added that "money spent on the RAF should not merely be an *addition* to army and navy expenditure but to some extent a substitute"; a seemingly wan demand in view of the fact that Beatty's battle cruisers alone would cost some thirty million pounds, or about twice the total 1921 Air Estimate figure.

In December 1919, Trenchard had bearded Beatty, and the even more unyielding First Lord, Leopold Amery, in the Admiralty to suggest an interregnum—"just twelve months to get started"—in order that the RAF's control of the naval air arm might justify itself. To Trenchard's surprise the First Sea Lord, abundantly confident that the navy's victory was in any case certain, agreed to the proposal. But now this armistice had expired, and with the findings of the Bonar Law Committee revealed, hostilities were resumed on a bitter level. The short term objective of both sides was the control of the Fleet Air Arm, which, since the dissolution of the Royal Naval Air Service in April 1918, had been under the control of the Air Ministry. Both Beatty and Trenchard knew that if this reverted to the Admiralty, the case for a third force would wither, so delicate were the roots of Trenchard's sapling service. But the front was much wider than this, and Trenchard and his supporters knew that they had to attack the whole conception of sea power in the post-war era. It was also a much less clearly defined front than that of the battle still raging in America. Trenchard never claimed publicly that the bomb would sink the battleship; the nearest he came to Mitchell's extremism was to state that aerial attacks are "a danger which the Fleet will find difficult to meet," and that the destructive power of the bomber was increasing more rapidly than the defensive power of the anti-aircraft gun. Beatty was equally unwilling wholly to commit himself. "In our opinion the capital ship remains the unit on which sea power is built," he said. "Nevertheless, it must be emphasised that, although the battleship remains, its type may be required to be altered. . . . It is even possible that the present battleship will change to one of a semi-submersible type, or even a flying type, but such types are visions of the far future. . . . The immediate abandonment of the capital ship in favour of a visionary scheme of aircraft and submarines would leave the British nation destitute of sea power. . . ."

But this coy reluctance to specify the battleship as the main *casus belli* did not obscure the issue to either contestant. Beatty and his Board understood as well as Trenchard that the Royal Navy bereft of its capital ships would be reduced to a secondary service, and that its place as defender of Britain's shores and her trade routes could be taken only by the flying service. Trenchard and the Air Ministry understood as well as Beatty that if they were to lose control of the Fleet's air arm their status would so shrivel that nothing could save them from extinction. An un-prejudiced observer had to put the odds in favour of Beatty and the battleship. The affection and trust of the nation still lay largely with the navy, and Beatty had in his favour the navy's war record, in which was embodied the figure of Beatty himself. Neither did Trenchard under-estimate the strength of the class foundations by which the navy was traditionally supported. Good breeding and influence ran together through the senior service; even King George V was a seaman and hated aeroplanes. It was popularly understood that airmen were rough, raffish and lower middle-class, and Trenchard knew that this sort of disparagement "could be more damaging than the enmity of admirals and generals and their camp followers at Westminster or Fleet Street."[10] Moreover, politics was a favourite retirement occupation for naval officers, and this helped to give a strong parliamentary bias in favour of the Admiralty. The Press, too, was almost solidly anti-Trenchard. Between them, the brothers Lords Rothermere and Northcliffe possessed an enormous influence through their control of many daily newspapers. Their prejudice against Trenchard and the RAF originated from Rothermere's experience as the first Secretary of State for Air, a post from which he was sacked, after Trenchard had resigned, by the deputy Prime Minister. These two Press lords coined the derisory term "Royal Ground Force" for use in their unremitting attacks on Trenchard's inefficiency after his return to the Air Ministry, and Rothermere himself put his signature to articles clearly aligning himself with the Admiralty cause for control of their own aircraft. Finally, Beatty could be said to have the powerful example of the United States and Japanese Navy Departments on his side. These two great powers, the only ones with big defence programmes in hand at the time, had evidently committed themselves wholeheartedly to the capital ship; and whatever interpretation Trenchard might make of the *Ostfriesland* trials, the official American report declared in substance that the battleship still ruled the oceans.

Against this weight of strength, Hugh Trenchard could gather seemingly meagre forces: the post-war achievements of the air arm, notably in subjugating tribes and chieftains in the Middle East—and even these redounded with accusations of barbarity by bomb and machine-gun against helpless encampments of tribal women and children; and the shrewdness, energy and single-minded faith in their cause of the body he led, with the outside support of politicians like Moore-Brabazon and Churchill. It took a little time for Trenchard to recognise that his one real chance of success lay in the over-confidence of the Admiralty in the outcome of the struggle. Beatty had first revealed this weakness in granting Trenchard the stay of execution at their December 1919 meeting, and notes of pomposity and transparent tendentiousness in Beatty's writings and speeches had since become more evident.

There was good reason for Beatty's attitude. By early 1922 it was true that he had lost his battle cruisers, but these had been abandoned as a result of the Washington Naval Conference, and Japan and the United States had made similar sacrifices. The Prime Minister, David Lloyd George, was determined to break up the air force and divide it between the War Office and Admiralty. His view was strictly that of the politician. But the professional opinion of the CIGS, Sir Henry Wilson, that the RAF was a force "coming from God knows where, dropping its bombs on God knows what, and going off God knows where," could not be disregarded. When Lloyd George fell from power as a result of the Chanak crisis over the Turko-Greek conflict, the new Premier Bonar Law inherited, with the continued turbulence in Iraq, a conviction that the RAF should be wound up. "The post may be abolished in a few weeks," he warned Samuel Hoare on offering him the Secretaryship of State for Air, the reason being that he had been advised that "the independent Air Force and the Air Ministry cost too much, and that there is everything to be said in peace time for going back to the old plan of navy and army control."[9] The RAF can be said to have been saved by the spirited sense of self-preservation of a junior minister faced with the loss of his first post before he was able to justify it. Hoare has told how he "listened enthralled to the words of the prophet" at his first meeting with Trenchard, and then, fired with sudden enthusiasm for a cause of which he had previously known little, determined to fight back against the seemingly hopeless odds. At a meeting of the Committee of Imperial Defence a few days after his appointment, Hoare listened to the members agreeing that the air force should go. Nervously, when only the formalities of disbandment remained to be discussed, he suggested to the Prime Minister that such a drastic decision at least qualified for an inquiry. To his surprise, the elder statesman, Lord Balfour, who was also present, was intrigued by this idea put forward by the young Minister. As a result of Balfour's powerful influence, a sub-committee was set up under Lord Salisbury to investigate relations between the Navy and the RAF and advise on the future organisation of the air service generally. Hoare thus obtained for Trenchard not only a stay of execution but a retiral for the consideration of fresh evidence.

During the hurly-burly of public accusation and counter-accusation, the two-way volleys of statistics, the lobbying, blandishments and exhortations that accompanied the taking of private evidence, both contestants threatened to quit so often that Bonar Law was moved to describe Trenchard as "something of an expert on resigning." Then, when the committee's conclusions, favouring Trenchard's case, were published in August 1923, Beatty and the Board of Admiralty informed the First Lord that they would all resign in a body rather than accept the report. There was a first-class national defence crisis, and

Trenchard took a long holiday while the trouble blew over—and the Cabinet confirmed the findings.

Trenchard could feel well satisfied with the result of the first four years of his second term as Chief of Air Staff. The Royal Air Force retained its independence, and retained under the strange dual-control system already operating, the Fleet Air Arm. In the words of Trenchard's Secretary of State, this "marked a turning point in the system of national defence." Hoare had indeed gained far more than he could have hoped for when he tentatively put forward his suggestion of an investigation at the meeting of the Committee of Imperial Defence. Great claims have also since been made by the partisans of both air and sea power that the findings of the Salisbury and Balfour Committees had a fundamental effect on the defence policy of Britain right up to the Second World War. Just how profound was the influence of these findings no one can ever say. Britain's air squadrons for home defence were increased, but this was certain to have taken place anyway in view of their ludicrous weakness and their disparity with the French air striking force at that time. It is possible, of course, that the navy's air arm under the direct and exclusive control of the Admiralty would have been developed as successfully as the aviation arms of the Japanese and United States navies; that an air corps similar to that efficiently developed by the American and French armies would have served Britain as well in the Battle of Britain as the RAF did.

The facts, at least, are now quite clear, even if they were not always clear at the time. Trenchard found that he was granted a seat of equal status with the other two services on the new Chiefs of Staff permanent sub-committee of the Committee of Imperial Defence; "but Trenchard was invariably the odd-man-out," and according to his biographer, "would soon learn that his position was not a comfortable, nor a particularly simple one."[10] The RAF remained the junior service, starved of money and resources, still socially an unattractive career for a young man; while the Admiralty could still claim the validity of H. A. L. Fisher's statement that the Bible and the Navy were the two greatest forces in British life. The Home Fleet was still the nation's first line of defence, and Beatty continued to get four times as much from the exchequer as the Air Ministry. Above all, Beatty was allowed to keep the two great battleships that had recently been laid down, and these —the *Nelson* and the *Rodney*—were little less formidable than the cancelled 1921 battle cruisers, were the largest and most powerful ever built in Britain, and their cost was more than the entire Air Estimates—which included civil aviation—for 1924. Not for another thirteen years, when rearmament in the face of new German power and aggression became a national issue and the strength of air attack had greatly increased, did the RAF begin to reach parity with the older services. And by that time, as a final irony and negation of the Salisbury and Balfour Committee's findings, the Admiralty had received back as a gift, and amid little controversy, the Fleet Air Arm.

It is, however, true to say that the outcome of the prolonged investigation revealed a wider appreciation of the power of the new arm than ever before, and its need of independence to grow its own roots; and that many of the shortcomings and benefits, the successes and failures of the RAF, the Fleet Air Arm and the Royal Navy, right up to the end of the Second World War, have been laid at the door of the Salisbury Committee Room.

It is still difficult to say whether in the long term it was Beatty's or Trenchard's service that won the exhausting 1923 duel. What is certain is that among the three great naval powers, the battleship had survived for one more term the fresh hazard with which it was threatened. Bombardment from the air, navalists the world over calculated, was no more than another threat to be added to that of the torpedo boat and submarine, and against which the provision could and would be made. This time armoured decks and multiple anti-aircraft guns were the answer. The rôle of the battleship had not changed. While shores remained to be guarded and trade routes kept open, the backbone of maritime power must continue to be vested in the giant gun platform. Such was the situation in 1924, when Britain, the United States and Japan were all adding to their battle fleets up to the limit of the self-imposed restrictions demanded by the Washington Naval Conference.

But in America one last, forlorn drama had still to be played out. In 1925 William Mitchell, surprisingly still Assistant Chief of the Air Service, continued to perform the part he had assigned for himself, even after he had failed to prove his case with the sinking of the *Ostfriesland* and other battleships in later trials. One of the longest dramatic performances in peace-time military history continued to retain its spirit and remarkable consistency.

Like Fisher, Mitchell had an abiding faith in the value of repetition and propaganda, and for nearly six years the script had required scarcely any modification. "Bombs sink battleships—and we've proved it. The battleship is dead. Naval power is dead. The aeroplane rules the world." The message was as simple as that. William Mitchell's performance eschewed the suppositions and qualifications that marked the London performance of the same play. But his audience interpreted the part in many different ways, seeing Mitchell variously as a saviour of his people from future enemies, as a huckster with a winged tract, as a warrior prophet who, with the fighting done, had only a divine message left to deliver; or simply as a phoney or a madman.

But William Mitchell never played the part of the comic or the fool, and if there was a swagger and an endearing conceit in all his performances, there was also a ringing note of honesty and conviction in the justice of his cause. As you follow his campaign through a never-ceasing round of speeches, articles and books, demonstrations, trials and conflicts with "swivel-chair administrators," "bone-headed admirals" and "reactionary, stiff-neck generals," you cannot fail to admire his doggedness, energy and selflessness. And he never once faltered or hinted at compromise.

The climax came in 1925. Since the *Ostfriesland* trials, Mitchell's behaviour as a serving army officer had become more and more recalcitrant, his language increasingly outspoken. No longer were Mitchell and the small body of loyal disciples who supported him in the air service—men like Henry Arnold, Ira C. Eaker, James Doolittle and Lewis Brereton—on speaking terms with those senior officers in the Navy and War Departments who most stoutly resisted their claims. Mitchell believed that the army and the navy, in order to minimise the strength of air power, were putting on spectacular flights with obsolete aircraft that were deliberately planned to fail. There had recently been several catastrophes which Mitchell believed could be traced to "sabotage." Then on 2 September, 1925, the airship *Shenandoah*, with forty-two aboard, slipped its mooring mast at Lakehurst, New Jersey, on a tour of state fairs. Early the following morning it crashed in an electric storm in the Ohio River valley. The tragic news was given to a nation that was already keyed up to anxiety by a prolonged search for a crew of navy airmen whose long-distance flying boat had been lost in the Pacific. At this time, and perhaps with a certain absence of tact, Secretary of the Navy Wilbur chose to make a speech which suggested that these series of disasters only proved once again that "the Atlantic and Pacific are still our best defences." Mitchell at once recognised the danger of the situation and retired to his office, deeply troubled and indignant, to draft out what he later described as his "bill of arrangement." There can be no doubt that he knew this would lead to court-martial, but he felt that the time had come for a last desperate attack on "the battleship kings." "He might as well have challenged the inspiration of the scriptures," was the bleak comment of that shrewd columnist, Clinton Gilbert.

When the indictment was handed out to the Press, it was found to be of some 6000 words and written in characteristic Mitchellese. "The accidents," he said, "were the direct results of incompetency, criminal negligence and almost treasonable administration," and he described the attitude of the two service departments towards aviation matters as "so disgusting in the last few years as to make any self-respecting person ashamed of the cloth he wears." He wrote of bluffing and bulldozing, of open falsehoods and disgusting performances. Two days later the *New York Times* correctly informed its readers that War Department officials were preparing Mitchell's court-martial.

The Washington public received Mitchell as a Hollywood star come to play the part of Custer at his last stand. He arrived on 25 September dressed in a loose fawn suit and a great sombrero-like hat with a soft cattleman's band round it, and swinging a light cane in his hand. "A fife and drum band of the American Legion, leading several hundred members of two posts displaying placards, augmented by a throng of other Mitchell fans, crowded the station to give him a rousing welcome. Hoisted on the shoulders of his admirers and carried through a lane of cheering spectators, Mitchell and his wife, who was nearly crushed by the mob, were finally rescued by Major H. H. Arnold who drove them off in his car. The following day, Mitchell was the guest at a barbecue given by the Society of Forty and Eight, a fun-making branch of the Legion. Mitchell was driven in a horse-drawn Victoria down Pennsylvania Avenue to the barbecue grounds, wearing a sky-blue poilu's cap and a blouse of the same colour."[7]

The off-stage junketings were matched only by the unrestrained language of those engaged in the court-martial that absorbed the attention of the whole country for some six weeks. Even the venerable old Admiral William Sims, who appeared as a defence witness, heard himself described as "opinionated, narrow-minded, hobby-horse riding, ego-maniacal." But only a small part of the time was taken up with the misdemeanours of William Mitchell. For the rest, it was the battleship itself, and the admirals whose faith still lay in the big-gun platform, that were on trial; although there was often confusion among those present as to who was the accused. "But you can bet your boots and spurs on one thing," one army officer was heard to say, "Billy Mitchell is having the time of his life." The result was inevitable. On 17 December, 1925, Mitchell was found guilty of insubordination and conduct prejudicial to discipline and was "suspended from rank, command and duty, with forfeiture of all pay and allowances for five years." Six weeks later he tendered his resignation as an officer in the United States Army.

4 . . . And a Swarm of Ants

In the two decades of anxious peace between the wars, there grew a terrible fear of a new "ultimate" weapon, the gravity-propelled high-explosive bomb. Science was seen to be out of hand, and the weapons—the high-explosive bomb, and its now forgotten twin-demon, the gas bomb—it was preparing would, it seemed to many people, next time destroy humanity.

The bomber's appearance over great cities like London, Paris and Cologne, left a strong impression on millions of people—who now recognised that the price of scientific advance was that no one and nothing would be safe in future wars. This piece of flattery to the power of the bomber was eagerly seized upon and encouraged to fuller growth by the proponents of air power. The bomber became the ultimate neurosis symptom in the crisis-ridden 1930s.

As always, ten years ahead of his time, Fisher had anticipated this obsession with the fear of explosive from the skies as long ago as January 1915 while he was still at the Admiralty. Then he had written[3] of "the terrible massacre resulting from the dropping of . . . twenty tons of explosive anywhere in the London area"; in 1944, cities a tenth the size of London were surviving a thousand tons in a night. By the mid-twenties the soothsayers were well into their stride. They included numbers of keenly intelligent students of warfare as well as interested partisans. One of the most trenchant was Brigadier-General P. R. C. Groves who wrote in a letter to *The Times* (27 July, 1923) of "aerial bombardment of the great cities and other nerve centres of this country. Such bombardment," he claimed, "might bring defeat within a few days." And in a series of special articles (which played their part in the Beatty-Trenchard battle) in the same newspaper in March 1922, he offered his opinion that bombs would destroy *all* the buildings and kill *all* the men, women and children of London.

This widespread fear of the high-explosive bomb was heightened by the bombing of cities in China, Spain and other countries. The dramatic use of high-explosive and gas bombs against the Abyssinians by the Italian Air Force, the successful hold over great areas of the Middle East and Indian frontier by the RAF, all helped to add credence to the belief that the bomber alone, with its apparent power to destroy a nation almost overnight, was the ultimate killer. Statisticians, as well as romantic prophets like H. G. Wells, failed to calculate that the greater area of modern cities is not made up of buildings at all, that with efficient repair squads urban services can soon be made to run again, that the output of factories, unless hit at a few vital points, is little affected by high-explosive from the air, that railway marshalling yards can be repaired almost as quickly as they can be damaged. These errors were faults of arithmetic. Even more satisfactory than the confounding of the statisticians was the discovery in the 1940s that people could not only withstand air bombardment, but that their will to resist the enemy was greatly strengthened by it.

In view of the conviction that the bomber would always get through (and finish any war in days), it is surprising that the "bomb versus battleship" controversy lasted for the full length of the between-the-wars period, and well into the war itself. But the same conditions, it was widely argued, did not necessarily apply to maritime war. Thus, the conjuration of the biggest-battleship biggest-gun, which had survived once again its threatened exposure after 1919, completed its cycle in uneasy companionship with that newer manifestation of the cult of the big bang. The bomber would wipe out cities and even annihilate mankind. But at sea the spell of the battleship had not yet been broken by 1937, when not only Britain, the United States and Japan, but France, Germany, and Italy as well were all busy hustling their shipyards for new super-dreadnoughts. It is hardly necessary to add that all these vessels were more powerful and formidable, protected by tougher steel, armed with more fearful ordnance, than ever before.

On 19 March, 1914, a patent application was made by two serving naval officers, the specification's preamble opening with these words: "We, Murray Fraser Sueter, Captain R.N., Director of Air Department, Admiralty, Whitehall, London, s.w., and Douglas Hyde Hyde-Thomson, Lieutenant R.N., of HMS *Vernon*, Portsmouth, in the County of Hants, do hereby declare the nature of this invention and what manner the same is to be performed, to be particularly described and ascertained in and by the following manner:

"The invention relates to seaplanes (i.e. aeroplanes designed to rise from and alight upon water) which carry and launch automobile torpedoes . . ."

The idea of using the aeroplane as a torpedo carrier seems first to have been considered some two years after Wilbur Wright's famous demonstrations at Le Mans, France, in 1908. The Germans contemplated dropping torpedoes from low-flying Zeppelins, and in 1911 an Italian officer, Captain Guidoni, actually succeeded in becoming airborne in a Farman biplane carrying a small torpedo weighing some 350 pounds. In Britain the leading pioneer was Murray Sueter, a brilliant naval officer who devoted the whole of his life to the struggle for recognition of suspect new weapons. He had been a wireless and torpedo specialist in the Royal Navy when such devices were generally regarded with contempt in the service. At the turn of the century, Sueter, more than any other single officer, had caused the Admiralty to experiment with a few Holland-type submarines. In 1908, when flying meant sporting balloon trips from Ranelagh on a summer afternoon, he had acquired the improbable title of Captain of Airships and already saw in the aeroplane a weapon that would revolutionise maritime warfare. To link the torpedo with this new swift craft—so much faster, more manoeuvrable and economical in cost and operation than the destroyer— seemed to Sueter the most natural thing in the world. After an exploratory trip to Germany with Colonel Mervyn O'Gorman, superintendent of the Royal Aircraft Factory at Farnborough, both officers being disguised as civilians, Sueter submitted a report to the Committee of Imperial

Defence pressing the claim of the airborne torpedo, to be carried preferably in a heavier-than-air machine.

The development of an aircraft sufficiently strong and powerful to carry a 14-inch Whitehead torpedo weighing some 800 pounds was a difficult problem in those days, and most people in the flying business shrugged off the idea as impossible. Sueter solved it with the help of four people. One of these was T. O. M. Sopwith, the young pioneer aircraft designer and manufacturer. The second was Louis Coatalen of the Sunbeam Company, a colourful and eccentric Franco-British mechanical engineer, who had already proved his uncanny skill at extracting greater power than seemed reasonable from the internal combustion engine. Coatalen succeeded in pushing the horsepower of his Sunbeam aero engine up to over 200 horsepower to provide the required lift. The third enthusiast who made the first British torpedo flight possible was Hyde-Thomson, who designed the launching apparatus and made the necessary modifications to the "mouldy" itself. Early in 1914 Squadron-Commander A. M. Longmore rose off the water in his experimental Sopwith seaplane and dropped the Royal Navy's first airborne torpedo.

Churchill and Fisher inspected this machine at Spithead just before the war, and when he became First Sea Lord again, Fisher encouraged the formation of a flight of them. In 1915 these three seaplanes were loaded up and sent out to try their paces in the Dardanelles operations. Between them they made three attacks, against a Turkish merchantman, an ammunition ship and a tug. Each sank at once. On the evidence of one hundred per cent success, in the throes of a war, it seemed likely that every encouragement would be given to a weapon that might become as successful as the surface and under-water torpedo carrier. Murray Sueter asked Sopwith to prepare the designs of a torpedo plane for quantity production, and a single prototype was completed. Then Sueter, an irascible and intolerant officer as well as a brilliant visionary, was relieved of his post as Director of Air Development, and his successor took no interest in the project. Fisher was gone from the Admiralty, Churchill was no longer First Lord. The little plane was later discovered strung up among the beams at the Sopwith works, and after much delay and consideration two hundred were ordered for the RNAS. They arrived too late to take any active part in the war.

Germany's interest in the torpedo plane was fleeting, too. A flight of Brandenburger twin-engined biplanes was formed at Zeebrugge in 1917, and on 1 May, 1917, two of them flew at low level across the North Sea and aimed their 17.7 inch torpedoes towards the British merchantman *Gena*. The *Gena* sank, but while she was going down she got her single light gun on to one of the Brandenburgers and shot it down. One of the two prisoners the *Gena's* boats picked out of the water was Richard Freude, Germany's Murray Sueter. Lacking his enthusiasm and drive, the Zeebrugge flight was soon disbanded.

There were other reasons for the failure of the torpedo plane to achieve any sort of recognition in the First World War. Navigation over the sea was still a chancy business, the weight of the torpedo restricted its use to a few specially constructed aircraft, whose range was short, the Board of Admiralty and the German Navy Department regarded the airship and aeroplane strictly as reconnaissance and spotting machines, and after 1 April, 1918 the navy lost control of the RNAS anyway. The new RAF was too preoccupied with the Western Front and the defence of London to give much serious thought to any aircraft as seemingly perilous and uncertain as a plane carrying a torpedo. Only a handful of officers and aircraft designers retained any interest in the weapon after the war. No public interest was shown in the machine, its numbers scarcely increased, though occasional voices of wisdom and foresight spoke out for it. This was understandable. The torpedo was a weapon that had brought Britain close to starvation; the torpedo was unrestricted sea warfare, innocent women and children drowning in the *Lusitania*, sailors left to struggle in the icy winter Atlantic. To a world satiated with death, the torpedo was a weapon of sickening horror. At the Washington Naval Conference proposals were put forward to ban both its old carrier, the submarine, and its new carrier, the torpedo plane. There was, also, in naval departments everywhere, the old unspoken and even unconscious reluctance to give any kind of encouragement to a weapon that might one day make not only battleships but all surface fighting ships obsolete.

But even after the passions and memories of the war had waned, and the navies of the world had made serious experiments with the torpedo plane, there were few signs of its acceptance. The most important reason for the slow, reluctant development of this swift and deadly sea weapon was its unsatisfactory power-image. In the 1920s, how could a wood-and-fabric biplane, its engine labouring under its load, and flying over the waves at a bare ninety mph with its uncertain torpedo hung from its belly, hope

83

to rival in its inspiration of strength and confidence a battle cruiser like the mighty *Hood*, of over 40,000 tons, with its eight tons' broadside of high-explosive shells ranging to nearly twenty miles?

Influential torpedo plane advocates on both sides of the Atlantic were so few that their appeals, when reported, seemed like the cries of churlish cranks. Murray Sueter, whose astonishing range of creative imagination had meanwhile helped to bring into being the tank, fought strenuous rearguard actions from the floor of the House of Commons, of which he was a member for twenty-four years. Referring to the Admiralty's refusal to put the torpedo plane into production before Jutland, he asserted time and again in the Commons that the torpedo bomber could have been decisive on the morning after the main engagement when Scheer was fleeing back to his base. "In making torpedo attacks by aircraft, no better place could have been chosen than the North Sea, with its low-lying clouds. . . . The torpedo machines could conceal themselves in the clouds, then, in making an attack, vol-plane down at an angle of forty-five degrees to the vertical . . . The machine would attack obliquely and retire obliquely, and it is obvious that the captain of guns would have only a few seconds to get their training on to frustrate an attack of this nature."[11]

One of Sueter's few staunch supporters was Percy Scott, who continued to hammer away in the columns of *The Times*, stating emphatically that the German fleet would never have got back at all if it had been attacked by Jellicoe with forty torpedo bombers. Another authority, who was less influential but equally energetic, was the naval architect and engineer, E. F. Spanner, who wrote a number of books on the superiority of the aeroplane over the surface fleet in any future war. Spanner's passionate advocacy led him to publish in 1926 a remarkably prophetic novel, little regarded at the time and quite forgotten to-day, called *The Broken Trident*. The story opens in a London-bound train. Two old friends, Dawson, the senior naval officer, traditionalist and "big ship" disciple, and Elton, the enthusiast for air power, argue their cases in the railway carriage. "I can't understand anyone," says Elton, "in these days of marvellously rapid progress, setting out to spend five to seven million pounds on a fighting unit which will take at least three years to complete, and which will be obsolete before she is finished." Dawson, the idealist and optimist, in turn pooh-poohs this suggestion. "If we do have another war, which God forbid, we shall look forward to having no more bloodthirsty submarine campaigns." When the two arrive in London they discover that war is indeed about to break out, the "New National Party" in Germany having delivered a twenty-four hours' ultimatum. At once Dawson joins his battleship and sails out under Admiral Kerson of the *Rameses* with the rest of the battle fleet to resist the foe. While cruising along the East Coast at night, the fleet is suddenly illuminated by a multitude of magnesium flares, turning darkness into day. From the flagship, the massed torpedo planes "looked like a string of tiny dots, for they were quite twenty miles away . . . No time to wait. Not a second can be wasted when an aeroplane, approaching at some 240 mph, shapes for attack. The enemy machines descended in a long line until they were just above the water."

Before sailing to meet the foe, the imperturbable Dawson had shrugged off scare talk about the torpedo plane. "They might annoy and irritate, even as a swarm of gnats might disturb the king of beasts . . . To-day will prove the thickness of the lion's skin. To-morrow will see his teeth biting into the stretch of German coastline." Instead, the torpedo planes, "noiseless in their approach," had gone straight for the sterns of the great vessels. "Within two minutes aerial torpedoes had crashed against the starboard quarters of each of the British battleships. . . . Explosions followed one another too rapidly for the ear to separate them. . . . Struck in a vital spot, with starboard propellers and rudder shattered, the vessels heeled slightly away from the explosion. . . . The Germans had wasted no time in attacks directed against the thousands of tons of armour which protected the vitals of the British warships," for "they knew that these essentials were entirely unprotected." Thus was the British battle fleet destroyed, and the nation overwhelmed.

So much for the visionaries and romantics. Reality lay down at Gosport, where the RAF had formed a Torpedo Development Unit and where during the late 'twenties and early 'thirties a four-months' torpedo training course, accommodating four or six pilots at a time, provided the Fleet Air Arm with a small nucleus of experienced torpedo plane pilots and observers. The training was of a remarkably high standard and the enthusiasm of this small, select body survived the absence of encouragement and the elementary *matériel* with which they had to make do. In 1926, there were just eighteen torpedo planes in the Fleet Air Arm. With these machines, new methods of attack were devised.

Attacks against the fleet target battleship *Agamemnon*, and later *Centurion*, were made at dawn or dusk from windward and with the sun behind, maintaining a bearing of forty-five degrees on the target and dropping their torpedoes as low as ten feet from the water at ranges of around a thousand yards. Later, experiments were made with head-on attacks and torpedoes with offset rudders that would describe a confusing circular course towards the target.

The activities of the torpedo plane on fleet manœuvres, and the calculated disparagement of its record on exercises—when battleships were often "torpedoed" with astonishing ease—closely followed those of its predecessor, the submarine, in the period before the First World War, and the torpedo boat earlier still; just as naval air officers lacked certain customary privileges and were regarded as socially inferior. It is hardly surprising that the torpedo plane's status failed to improve. The RAF, which still controlled naval aircraft, remained chiefly interested in the bomb as a weapon of attack at sea and viewed the torpedo as an expensive weapon, its carrier as slow, cumbersome and vulnerable. To the Admiralty, the aeroplane still remained as an auxiliary weapon of doubtful reliability. Further confidence in the battle fleet's ability to ward off enemy air attack, from torpedo planes or bombers, was instilled by the development of the anti-aircraft gun, notably the multi-barrelled two-pounder pom-pom, the equivalent of the earlier Gatling and Nordenfeld. Almost word for word, the same arguments were used to destroy verbally the torpedo plane in the 1930s as spokesmen for the big battle-ship school had used forty years before to disparage the torpedo boat. From the quick-firing guns of the ironclad, the torpedo boat, it had been said, "would be under fire from about 3000 yards up to 600 yards. . . . It is not likely that torpedo boats will be sent against intact battle-ships, whose quickfirers are in good order and whose gunners are unshaken. . . . The torpedo boat lacks protection, as its only defence is its diminutive size and very high speed, and it is valueless for offence outside five hundred yards. . . . The torpedo has a limited range, and as long as the fleets fight at a distance it cannot be used, whilst even at close quarters it is somewhat uncertain."[12] Thirty-five years later, a party of officials and reporters invited to Portsmouth to witness a demonstration of the new "pom-pom" gun was "left pretty breathless," according to Admiral Sir Roger Keyes's report to the Commons on this "antidote to the aircraft," this "wonder anti-aircraft gun." "The new weapon has revolutionised the navy's methods of dealing with low-flying bombing aircraft and torpedo planes," the *Daily Telegraph*'s naval correspondent assured his readers. "Its range far exceeds that at which a torpedo plane could hope to launch a successful attack. The stream of shells lashing the water . . . sets up a barrage through which no machine could pass." Figures in positions of authority or great influence, like Lord Curzon and Admiral Sir Herbert Richmond, stressed again and again that the torpedo plane had affected neither the rôle nor the security of the battle-ship. "It is necessary . . . not to make the same over-estimation of the flying torpedo craft as has been made in earlier times of the surface types," wrote Admiral Richmond in his scholarly analysis *Sea Power in the Modern World*. "Modern ships can produce a volume of defensive fire . . . that will drive aircraft to such a height that the efficiency and accuracy of their attacking weapons will be seriously impaired," the Parliamentary Secretary to the Admiralty, Mr. Geoffrey Shakespeare, assured the House six months before war broke out. The danger to the attacking crew and the ability of the target to avoid the oncoming torpedo were referred to in identical terms by big gun navalists in 1890, 1910 and 1930; only the carrier changed, from torpedo boat to submarine to torpedo plane.

Through it all—through control by the navy until 1918, through control by the RAF until 1937, and then once again under an Admiralty still lacking much enthusiasm for the airborne torpedo carrier—the tiny nucleus of enthusiasts continued to refine their skill, always with pitiably out-dated equipment.

In America the *matériel* situation was a little better. Britain may have pioneered the aircraft carrier, but in the *Lexington* and *Saratoga* the United States Navy had the most advanced carriers in the world, and the planes that flew from them in the 1930s, like the Curtiss Hawk fighter, with retractable undercarriage and a speed of 250 mph, made the British Fleet Air Arm machines look like relics from the First World War; which indeed most of them were. In 1935, while Lord Londonderry was announcing with some pride that nineteen new aircraft would be added to the Fleet Air Arm that year (eighteen had been added between 1929 and 1932), the American Chief of Naval Operations, Admiral William Standley, was reporting to the House of Representatives Naval Committee in Washington: "Britain has virtually no air force in the navy," he said. "I have just been over there and I know. Operations from her aircraft carriers are so elementary in type and character that

89

she is now doing some of the things we did ten years ago."
The wonder was that there was not the same wide gap in
the morale between the British and American naval air
services.

The most important reason for the greater attention that
had finally been given to the flying branch of the United
States Navy, was the evidence from across the Pacific that
the Japanese were putting their faith in air attack, by both
bomb and torpedo, to compensate for their disparity in
capital ships with America, as controlled by the Washington Naval Treaty. Even before the First World War, while
men like Eugene Ely in America and Samson in Britain
were experimenting with seaplanes and ship launchings,
the Japanese Navy was buying aircraft from Europe and
carrying out its own trials. The fact that the casualty rate
among pilots was so excessive that nearly all Japan's pioneer
airmen were dead by 1914, in no way discouraged these
efforts, and in 1916 the Japanese air service received its
first appropriation of £60,000. The leading advocate was
Isoroku Yamamoto, who as early as 1915 was declaring
in an interview, "The most important ship of the future will
be a ship to carry aeroplanes."[13] In 1918, the Japanese air
service received £154,000, and in the following year the
appropriation was increased by an admiring American of
great wealth, who gave the Japanese Government £18,000
"with the request that it be devoted to the purchase of
flying machines and the training of pilots." The Japanese
possessed, in his opinion, "qualities which ought to make
them the finest aviators in the world."[14] The Japanese
readily fell in with this request, and among other British
firms, the Blackburn company benefited by a sale of a

number of Napier-engined Dart torpedo planes. The British Government pulled its weight, too. In 1923, at the request of the Imperial Japanese Navy, an advisory British Naval, Mission comprising former RNAS pilots, was sent out to Tokyo to give what help they could.

Yamamoto, Suetsugu and the other leading Japanese air power enthusiasts suffered the same sort of attacks as Mitchell and Arnold, Trenchard and the Salmond brothers experienced in the U.S.A. and Britain. Within the Navy Department, the battle was waged intermittently for twenty years, and the same arguments that were used in London and Washington were heard behind closed conference chamber doors in Tokyo and Kure. There was, however, one significant difference. Always Yamamoto laid special emphasis on the power of the torpedo plane. "How can you expect to destroy a battleship except with a battleship?" he must have often been asked. And always his reply was, "With torpedo planes. You know the proverb: 'The fiercest serpent may be overcome by a swarm of ants.' "[13]

The Japanese Navy never forgot that early demonstration of the power of the torpedo put on by the father of the service, Admiral Togo himself, in 1904 at Port Arthur. In half an hour the balance of naval power in the Far East had been tipped in their favour by a handful of Whiteheads. Whatever disputes occurred, in the years before Japan once again went to war in the Pacific, as to the most effective means of delivering the torpedo, the instrument of destruction itself never fell from favour. Both in Britain and Japan experiments were made during the First World War with new forms of propulsion that would raise the speed, range and carrying-capacity of the automobile torpedo.

Oxygen fuel was the most favoured, and it was also the most dangerous. In the Royal Navy these experiments continued well into the 1920s, before the decision was made to revert to safer and more predictable compressed air. The Japanese Navy Department was more persistent, and by 1923, when for reasons of economy work was halted, they were well on the way to success. A Japanese suicide human-torpedo pilot who survived the war has told of the false report from a naval officer visiting Portsmouth that the Royal Navy had oxygen-powered torpedoes in service in 1927. "While touring the battleship HMS *Rodney* he noticed an odd-looking apparatus on one of her decks. His experienced eye told him at once it was an oxygen generator, but he pretended to give it little notice. A few days later he heard that the *Rodney*, which had torpedo tubes mounted below her waterline, like many other battleships of her day, was going to run a torpedo test."[15] The Japanese officer contrived to witness this test, and incorrectly presumed from his observations that the torpedoes were oxygen-impelled. His alarmed report decided the Japanese Navy Department to renew their efforts to solve the earlier problems, and as a result, a navy that had developed until then largely by imitation, made an epochal step forward and far in advance of its old tutors.

The official American naval historian, Samuel Eliot Morison, has told how the Japanese secretly and tirelessly strove to perfect first an oxygen-enriched and then a fully oxygen-powered torpedo between 1928 and 1933; "an outstanding technical achievement."[16] The Type 95 Mk II had a diameter of twenty-four inches, a length of nearly thirty feet, a speed of forty-nine knots, at a range of 5760 yards. Its total weight was 6000 lb., and the charge in its warhead weighed 1210 lbs. It made every other torpedo in the world obsolete overnight; but unlike almost every British naval invention of the twentieth century—such as the magnetic mine of the First World War and the multiple pom-pom so widely publicised at its Portsmouth demonstration—Japan kept her priceless discovery to herself. Even greater importance was attached to torpedo training and development in the following seven years. While the Royal Navy and the United States Navy placed dummy cork warheads on their practice torpedoes and patiently searched for their expended weapons after exercises, the Japanese Navy exploded them with a lavish disregard for their cost. While their future foes dropped sand bombs on target battleships and debilitated themselves in controversy over the results, the Imperial Japanese Navy sent their old battleships *Satsuma* and *Aki* to the bottom with three oxygen torpedoes exploding with twice the force of any American or British "tin fish." By 1941, most Japanese destroyers and submarines were equipped with the infamous "Long Lance," a diabolical underwater killer, with a range of 22,000 yards, that caused such destruction and dismay in the Pacific during the opening months of the war.

In 1941, too, Isoroku Yamamoto had under his command the aircraft carriers he had first campaigned for twenty-five years earlier; nine of them, more than any other naval power in the world. His air crews were the most experienced and skilful. Crews of land-based torpedo planes consistently achieved an average of seventy-four per cent hits against battleships on manœuvres, and even in war this figure was officially estimated to become not less than twenty-five per

93

cent. All of them had been through a training that was marked by extreme physical rigour, monastical isolation, and spiritual dedication. Morison describes the ruthlessness of the Imperial Navy's exercises in cold northern waters, far from possible observation, during which perhaps a hundred deaths from operational accidents were not unusual; and this same authority quotes one of the training pamphlets: ". . . with a tenacious and tireless spirit we are striving to reach a superhuman degree of skill and perfect fighting efficiency. . . ." Few of them failed to reach this standard.

But even in Japan the big-gun school of strategy had won major victories in the years of peace and preparation. The *Musashi* and *Yamato*, of 75,500 tons full load displacement and with a main battery of 18.1 inch guns represented the fulfilment of the dreams of the most relentless battleship advocates: unsurpassed super-super-dreadnoughts. (Later, they were both to fall victim to United States Navy torpedoes.)

In reviewing the weight of confidence vested in the big gun in 1941, differing judgments made by the three greatest naval nations can now be recognised. Japan had the greatest faith in the destructive power of the plane, and especially the torpedo carrier, while accepting the need for the big-gun platform until the enemy battle fleet was destroyed by the torpedo, from destroyers, submarines or planes. The United States Navy's attack strength still lay primarily in the battleship, of which there were ten building or completing in American yards in the summer of 1941, at a cost of around one hundred million dollars apiece. Here maritime power still rested on a single pillar,

traditionally architected, although a second supporting strut
was discernible. There were even senior officers to be found
in Washington and with the fleet who believed that the
Pacific naval war would be fought mainly in the air and under
the ocean; but they made up a small minority, their fore-
casts still unheeded. The "battlewagon" remained the prime
arbiter.

At the renewal of her war with Germany, in 1939, the
maritime policy of the oldest naval power lacked the fine
shades of compromise, between the relative destructive
power of the big gun and the aeroplane, accepted in Japan
and the United States. The total complement of the Royal
Navy's carriers was 189 aircraft, of which 147 were obsolete
Swordfish planes, combining the duties of spotting,
reconnaissance and torpedo-dropping. The air crews
were game, gallant and skilful. But the twelve Sea Gladiator
single-seater fighters with which they were provided to
ward off enemy attack were fixed-undercarriage biplanes
markedly slower than German medium bombers. A big
programme of carrier building was in hand, but there was
no hint that this expenditure was to alter the solidly-
entrenched strategical position allotted to the fleet's aircraft.
They were to spot the fall of shot for the gunners, help
to protect the fleet against submarine and air attack,
reconnoitre, and shadow the enemy after sighting. These
functions had not altered since 1918, when the old RNAS
had been swallowed up by the RAF. The only suggestion
that the aeroplane had acquired over the past twenty years
any useful powers of destruction was to be found in its
additional duty to "Attack by striking forces on a faster
enemy attempting to escape battle, thus reducing his speed

to enable our surface ships to come into action."[17] (There were occasions, for example pursuing against a very high wind fast Italian cruisers, when even this offensive function was denied them as the Swordfish loaded with a torpedo showed scarcely any superiority in speed.)

In 1939 the British naval plane was not intended primarily for striking, and the carrier's rôle was still to help the fleet as an auxiliary, to prevent itself from being sunk (which was widely expected in the RAF and in some naval quarters), to escort important convoys, and to hunt submarines. The important duty of the aircraft, of spotting the fall of shell for the capital ships, underlined once again the continued paramountcy of the big gun in the Royal Navy.

The muscles of maritime power still flexed from the spine of the capital ship. Two of these vessels had been designed eighteen years before, and the other thirteen dated back to the First World War and before. The inadequacy of this battle fleet had been recognised by the Board of Admiralty for many years, and under the recent rearmament programme five more battleships had been laid down. It was one of these battleships that was to succumb, soon after its completion, to the torpedoes of Japanese naval aircraft in the Battle of the Gulf of Siam; and, amid a welter of recrimination, spell at last the end of the battleship as a weapon in maritime warfare.

The story of how this battleship came to be built, how it came to be off the coast of Malaya on the morning of 10 December, 1941, and how it was destroyed, is told in the following pages.

5 *The Ships*

J UST ONE MONTH after King Edward VIII's abdication in December 1936, a battleship which would carry the name of his former title was laid down by the shipbuilding firm of Cammell Laird at Birkenhead. HMS *Prince of Wales*, one of the first battleships to be built in Britain for fifteen years, signalled the emergence of the Royal Navy from the defence policy confusion of the 1930s, under which it had suffered every infliction from financial strangulation and political vacillation, to a mutiny. Since David Beatty had accepted the surrender of the High Seas Fleet in 1918, it had survived the attempts to disparage its *matériel* and functions by the air power extremists, its starvation of funds by the Treasury, and its necessity for existence at all by the powerful pacifist groups. By 1936, as has been told, the Royal Navy possessed only two modern battleships, and both cruiser and flotilla strength were far below the minimum requirements of the Board.

By 1936 the battleship's struggle to justify its existence had lasted for over fifty years. They were so much more expensive than any other weapon and they were so much more tangible and comprehensible than, say, military arsenals and bases, depots and supplies, that battleships were always certain of catching public attention. The cost of a battleship could be reckoned in shillings per head of the population. Also because of its size, its grandeur, its power to inflict and resist destruction, and because of the deep emotions it aroused, the battleship continued to retain for its lifetime a capacity for causing controversy.

Between the wars there were only two periods of battleship building among the naval powers. The bombing trials, committee investigations and verbal violence aroused in Britain and America by the first have already been mentioned. From this period the battleship emerged with its official status scarcely diminished. Its size and cost, however, had reached such an intolerable level that the great powers signed with relief the Washington Treaty restricting their construction for ten years. By the time the "naval holiday" was nearing its end, the nations' finances were in such a precarious situation that they could not afford new battleships anyway. The great crash and the slump succeeded where the frenzied efforts of Mitchell, Arnold, and Sims, Trenchard, Fisher, and Scott and the other extreme advocates of air power had failed to destroy the capital ship's reputation. Empty exchequers were better proof of the obsolescence of the battleship than bombs on the target ships *Ostfriesland* and *Agamemnon*. This curious strategic perversion was typified by a passage in a British Government memorandum issued on 4 February, 1930. "In the opinion of His Majesty's Government," it stated, "the battleship, in view of its tremendous size and cost, is of doubtful utility, and the Government would wish to see an agreement by which the battleship would in due time disappear altogether from the fleets of the world." The other naval powers were in no position to dispute this

judgment, and in fact were in the throes of a naval conference in London which was to keep the world's shipyards
empty of big naval keels for a further five years. Not only
did Britain, the United States and Japan agree to abstain
from battleship building until the end of 1936, but between
them they agreed to dispose of ten of their existing capital
ships, which never cost less than a quarter million pounds
annually each, merely to maintain. "The conclusion that
the battleship had better be regarded as an obsolete vessel"
by the expiry date of the new treaty was a state of affairs
that the Prime Minister, Ramsay MacDonald, eagerly
hoped for, he said in the House of Commons on 15 May,
1930.

In 1930, then, admiralties and navy departments all over
the world were being told that they would get no reinforcements nor even replacements for their ageing battle fleets.
"The Government considers (battleships) a very doubtful
proposition in view of their size and cost, and of the development of the efficiency of air and submarine attack," an
article in *The Times* on 8 February, 1930 stated. Authori-
tative opinion gave as the reason for this *volte face* the
belated acceptance of the facts of air power. This seemed
to them a reasonable enough conclusion. Its fallacy, and
the remarkable strength and power of recovery of the
battleship image, became clear only when a decision for war
was made by some great powers and its likelihood was
accepted by others. Already by 1935, when a third
naval conference was convened in London, the runners
in the new arms race were limbering up, and Ramsay
MacDonald's old hopes for the abolition of the capital ship
altogether rapidly faded. Instead, the delegates from the

naval powers began to wrangle about such niceties as the limitations of future gun calibres, and the desirability of allowing aircraft catapults on the decks of battleships. The result was hardly a mortal blow to the traditionalists and big-gun-big-ship enthusiasts. Guns were to be limited to 14-inch, displacement to 35,000 tons; numbers unlimited. With restraints relaxed, with nervous governments once again filling the arms factories' order books (and the slump receding rapidly in consequence), and the threat of air power still unresolved, policy decisions of five years earlier were conveniently forgotten. In Germany, Italy, Japan, France, Britain and the United States, the battleship, like some ageing matinée idol intent on a come-back, slipped once again into its rôle as the most fearful individual expression of man's needs to intimidate his neighbours.

In Britain, the construction of the *Prince of Wales* and her four sister ships was not put in hand without arousing the customary disturbance; they were, after all, going to cost the taxpayer over £50 million. But this time, instead of the conflict being a straight fight between the pro- and anti-battleship schools, there were four shades of opinion represented by four antagonists. First there were the compromisers, led by Admiral Sir Herbert Richmond, who preached the case for the small battleship. They got the ready support of vacillating politicians like MacDonald, and were the darlings of the Treasury. Then there were the successors to Fisher and Scott, now more refined in their dialectics, intellectual strategists in the tradition of Mahan and Corbett. Among these was Commander Russell Grenfell, one of the very few who saw in the airborne torpedo the most effective weapon against the capital ship and recognised that aircaft had extended their operating range since 1918. "The point seems to have been reached," he wrote in 1938, "where fleets cannot be kept clear of shore-based aircraft, and will have to put up with air attack in their bases if they are to continue to exercise their proper functions."[24] There was, Grenfell argued, "an increasing tendency to think more of preserving the great ship from damage than of using her to damage the enemy . . . to think of the battleship in terms of 'can we keep her safe?' than of 'can she sink the enemy?'" He calculated that Britain's battle fleet now required auxiliary and protecting vessels with a tonnage totalling thirty-seven per cent of its own displacement, whereas at Trafalgar the figure was only eight per cent. Grenfell liked to quote the findings of the 1871 Committee on the Design of Warships which stated that "a simple and perhaps, under ordinary circumstances, a safe method by which the requirements of the British Navy may from time to time be estimated, is to watch carefully the progress of other nations in designing and constructing ships of war, and to take care that our own fleet shall be more than equal in number and power of its ships to that actually at the disposal of any other nation." It seemed to him that, if the justification for the Admiralty's faith in five new battleships "is that the American, Japanese, German, French and Italian Admiralties profess the same faith, how can we be sure that, for instance, the American policy is not determined by the apparent conviction of the French, Italian, German and Japanese: and so on . . ." The battleship's function, he thought, "has practically been reduced to that of watching the movements of the corresponding great ships of an enemy and bringing them to action if they offer an opportunity for doing so."

Colonel J. T. C. Moore-Brabazon, for long an air power advocate, put the case more sweepingly in the House of Commons on 10 November, 1936. "I have read with great interest the pamphlet[19] which justifies, apparently, the construction (of new battleships) on the basis that other people are building battleships, and we should do the same. I am not prepared to dispute that," he said. "Let the Admiralty have their battleships and take them as far away as possible so that they do not come to any harm —that is what they always do with battleships. But I should like the House to notice the somewhat unconscious humour of the Admiralty, that although nobody else can do any harm to our battleships from the air, they are keen to get a larger air fleet to harm enemy battleships."

The most influential member of the intellectual school who opposed the building of the new battleships was Captain B. H. Liddell Hart, the military correspondent of *The Times*, whose field of interest was, of course, much wider than Grenfell's. Like Commander Grenfell, he pressed for the construction of more aircraft carriers and flotilla craft—and liked to remind his readers of the Mediterranean Fleet's withdrawal from Malta during the height of the 1935 Abyssinian crisis for fear of Italian air attack. This suggested to him that the question of whether a bomb could sink a battleship was largely academic. What really mattered was whether the threat of destruction or crippling from the air could prevent the battleship from carrying out its strategic rôle. Liddell Hart has always possessed to a remarkable degree the power to cast aside long-established beliefs and prejudices, to cut through the verbiage of official reports, to review the lessons of past policies and conflicts; then to bring to bear on every problem a penetrating judgment that often surprises by its simplicity. With these unusual assets, he combines a real talent for clarity and economy as a writer. At this period, for example, he wrote of the battleship dilemma:

"It is not that generals and admirals are incompetent, but that the task has passed beyond their competence. Their limitations are due not to a congenital stupidity—as a disillusioned public is apt to assume—but to the growth of science, which has upset the foundations of their technique. They are like men who cling to their little wooden huts in an earthquake. The only way of salvation would be to get out in the open—to survey the problems in complete detachment and from the widest point of view.

"But a scientific habit of thought is the least thing that military education and training have fostered. Perhaps that is an unalterable condition, for the services might hardly survive if they parted company with sentiment— if the bulk of their members detached themselves from the loyalties which are incompatible with the single-minded loyalty to truth that science demands."[20]

The extreme opposite end of the scale was represented by an ultra-reactionary fringe who viewed the continuing attacks on the battle fleet almost as the treacherous sniping by heathen rebels of Christian crusaders. Liddell Hart was frequently counter-attacked as one of these insurgents. "You have evidently been crammed up, as I fear that both the Government and the public at home have, by the air propaganda," he was told in a letter from the GOC one of the most important overseas army commands. "There is only one way in which the air can win a war and that is by bombing women and children; and that will never bring a great nation to its knees, but only inferior people. You know perfectly well that the navy laughs at the air now. They have got protected decks, and with their 'blisters' and multiple machine-guns . . . they don't fear them in the slightest."

It was "the indecency of aerial bombardment" that dismayed another officer, Captain Bernard Acworth, R.N. On the other hand he argued that it was untrue that "in the past few years the destructiveness of explosives has been increased. 1,413 people might have been killed in 103 bombing attacks in the last war, but nothing worse was to be expected in the future. And if war ever came to frightfulness again, "the long-range guns of the navy could flatten out more towns, and kill and maim more women and children in one day's coastwise cruise, than all the squadrons of aeroplanes we are ever likely to possess could manage in all the flights they could ever make."[21] Captain Acworth liked to quote from A. H. Pollen. "No weapon or device can supplant the gun. The belief, carefully fostered in the public mind, that huge bombs will rain down on battleships is childish, for the simple reason that, apart from aiming disabilities, such bombs cannot be lifted or conveyed in quantity to the scene of action." For this reason, Acworth considered that means of defence against aircraft attack by bomb or torpedo were unnecessary. "Perhaps the vital need of the navy to-day is to take up the torpedo by the gills, so to speak, and to look this pretentious bugbear squarely in the mouth. It will assuredly be found, on closer inspection, that its teeth are false—that it carries in its mouth, in fact, a 'denture.' " Anti-torpedo bulges on battleships were, therefore, "strategically devastating," the "welter of mechanical contrivances" aesthetically offensive to those who still spared a thought for the line and grace of a fine vessel; which had vanished "to give place to erections and accretions which are as hideous as they are retrograde."

The wireless gear, the elaborate instruments, the spotting and reconnaissance aircraft and its catapult, and the batteries of anti-aircraft guns and anti-torpedo protection deplored by Captain Acworth, were, however, accepted as necessary by yet another committee of experts which sat in 1936 to decide whether the battleship still had a place in the nation's defence system, whether the country should take advantage of the end of the "battleship holiday" that had already lasted fourteen years, to lay down five more monster super-dreadnoughts. Judgment was fraught with massive imponderables. It was not only that these five were calculated to cost more than any other single year's programme of armoured ships in the history of the Royal Navy, even in the full tilt of the pre-1914 naval race. Nor that, since then, the power of the battleship to fill its rôle and survive the new weapons of maritime war had become much more questionable. The long break in heavy naval shipbuilding following the Washington Treaty, and then the slump, had caused the disbandment of design teams, the dispersal of specialised labour, and a serious break in the entire tradition of big-ship construction, once a major industry. The building of five 35,000 ton battleships demanded not only the recruitment of thousands of skilled men from other armament occupations, but the diversion of tens of thousands of tons of special quality steel, and the serious disruption of ordnance factories. It was the most momentous decision British defence organisation had to take in the whole period of rearmament leading to the Second World War.

The last of the committees to sit in judgment on the battleship was presided over by Lord Inskip, Minister for Co-ordination of Defence, and had, besides the Chairman, Malcolm MacDonald and Lord Runciman, President of the Board of Trade. Their expert advisers were the First Sea Lord, Lord Chatfield, and the Chief of Air Staff, Air Chief Marshal Sir Edward Ellington. Among the witnesses called were Murray Sueter, Herbert Richmond and Sir Eustace Tennyson-D'Eyncourt, designer of Britain's last battleships, *Nelson* and *Rodney*. These three represented, respectively, the anti-battleship, pro-small-battleship, and traditional groups. There was a slight bias in favour of the air-power school in the choice of witnesses. Moore-Brabazon and Winston Churchill declined to appear.

It is not interesting nor necessary to follow the elaborate processes of thought passed through by this committee. Much of the evidence considered was identical to that taken by previous committees, in Britain and America. All the *Ostfriesland* trials' results were looked at again in detail, for the reason that there had never since been such a thorough investigation into the vulnerability of the battleship to the bomb. The effectiveness of anti-aircraft fire "was the most difficult part of the inquiry to assess." The Admiralty made clear its belief in the modern battleship, claiming that the "capital ship of the future can be so designed as to distribution of her armour on decks and sides, and as to interior sub-division, that she will not be subject to fatal damage from the air." Bombs were only like plunging long-range fire from guns. The committee expressed doubt about the ability of aircraft to operate far from their bases over the sea, the darkness, poor weather and difficulties of navigation being severe handicaps. For this reason, it was thought desirable in a future war for naval forces supported by capital ships to operate in the "wide seas," well out of range of aircraft. Many other recommendations were made by the Inskip Committee, touching on the need to defend bases adequately, to carry out further experiments with bombs on battleships, and to foster closer collaboration between the services. There appeared to be no suggestion of contradiction in their conclusions that no capital ship could be built so as to be indestructible from air bombing, and that "we need ships equal in fighting power to those to which they may be opposed." The torpedo bomber was scarcely mentioned; the Admiralty, it seemed, had "developed special weapons to deal with this form of attack."

Finally, the cost was brushed aside. No other great naval power proposes to do away with capital ships; why should we, with most to lose, be the first to do so? "The advocates of the extreme air view would wish this country to build no capital ships (other powers still continuing to build them). If their theories turn out well-founded, we have wasted money; if ill-founded, we would, in putting them to the test, have lost the Empire."

Britain did not dare to face the prospect of war at sea without five new battleships, regardless of their cost. That is how the *Prince of Wales* and her four sisters came to be laid down in 1937, to represent the British team in the new battleship race.

The origins of HMS *Repulse*, the other capital ship with whose destruction this book is finally concerned, go back to the days of Fisher, and to his strategic obsession, the Baltic Project. Fisher's uncanny foresight perceived the likelihood of military stalemate on the Western Front when most people were still expecting "the boys to be home for Christmas" in 1914. To forestall this, Fisher preached for all his worth a plan for landing an army on the German Pomeranian coast, and a *blitzkrieg* 90-miles rush to the German capital. In this swift, daring, flank attack Fisher saw our only salvation from the horrors of trench warfare. The navy could be relied upon for safe escort of the invading army, which would travel in "huge amphibian monsters . . . ploughing their way in thousands like huge hippopotami across the North Sea and crawling impregnable up the beaches and so inland." For this Baltic operation, the navy would also need vessels with light draught, very high speed, and the heaviest guns available; the very apotheosis of his beloved battle cruisers. As First Sea Lord and *primum mobile* of the recent successful destruction of von Spee's marauding force by his battle cruisers off the Falkland Islands, Fisher was able to obtain Cabinet authority to redesign two "R" class battleships to his own "Baltic" formula: 32 knots, six 15-inch guns and the thinnest sheathing of armour plate. The power of the torpedo, however, was acknowledged by a "bulge" containing compartments of oil and air which extended to a width of fourteen feet and for almost the whole length of the vessel. John Brown

& Co. on the Clyde laid down the *Repulse* in January 1915, and by dint of the most strenuous efforts, had her in the water less than a year later. But by the time she was completed in August 1916, Jutland had been fought and the battle cruiser, from being the most highly esteemed big ship in the Royal Navy, had declined almost to the "white elephant" class because of the apparently effortless destruction of three of her kind by German shell. Fisher, by this time in the wilderness, could only protest ineffectually that his battle cruisers were never intended to fight in the line and engage in prolonged gun duels, and that to pack more armour plate on their hulls and decks was to destroy their design balance and suggest the playing of an improper rôle. But when the lovely *Repulse* with her simple classic line and her forward sheer and flare, joined the Grand Fleet, she was sent packing like an unsuitably dressed débutante for her protection to be attended to.

At least the *Repulse* could claim the privilege of firing her guns in anger and at enemy capital ships after Jutland, which was more than all but a handful of the vessels of the Grand Fleet could record. In company with her sister ship, *Renown*, and two other battle cruisers, she fought a brief mist-and-smoke obscured duel with four heavy German units between Horn Reef and Terschelling: a typical North Sea abortive action. And one other distinction fell to the ship before the surrender. On 1 October, 1917, Flight Commander F. J. Rutland DSC, R.N., flew for the first time a fighter plane experimentally off a platform secured over two of her main guns, thus providing her with some sort of protection against the new threat from the air. *Repulse*'s life precisely spanned the capital ship's period of insecurity from the menace of the aircraft, from its first recognition to her own sinking twenty-four years later; the first capital ship ever to be sunk at sea by aircraft.

With the war over, and the decision made against scrapping her, *Repulse* was taken in hand for a major refit that cost nearly a million pounds and resulted in her being weighed down with over a thousand tons of additional armour plate. Thus HMS *Repulse* entered the air age, with an inch or two of hardened steel on her decks, four anti-aircraft guns, and an aeroplane poised symbolically on her third big-gun turret.

Her years of peace, like those of her few surviving cohorts, were taken up with routine duties in home and Mediterranean waters, and the showing of the flag in distant places. There was a visit to Rio de Janeiro for the Brazilian centenary celebrations in 1922; a world cruise lasting nearly a year from September 1923, taking in the West Indies, the major Dominions, and Singapore, then in a less anxious condition than when she next visited the city sixteen years later; and another journey to South America and South Africa, this time with the Prince of Wales as a royal guest of honour. A further attempt to strengthen her defences against bomb and torpedo was made at Portsmouth from 1934 to 1936. When she emerged from dockyard hands this time, HMS "Repair," as she was uncharitably nicknamed by the fleet, had a hangar abaft her second funnel and a pair of cranes for handling her spotting and reconnaissance planes on to the catapult. Her old First World War anti-aircraft guns were replaced by six four-inch weapons in pairs, two formidable four-barrel two-pounder anti-aircraft guns further increased her power to resist air assault, and four of the highly-praised eight-barrel pom-poms were assigned to her. Unfortunately, there was a heavy run on these in the fleet and she got only two of them. But, aside from the anachronistic aircraft cranes, she was as lovely a vessel as ever when she began her second war in September 1939.

To one of the ship's company who had served in 1918, the battle fleet might have been suspended in time for the years of peace. Twelve out of fifteen of the capital ships had been with Beatty's Grand Fleet; and from a distance the multiple pom-poms were indiscernible. Up at Loch Ewe and Scapa Flow, the stark, threatening silhouettes of the battleships and battle cruisers touched with grey the grey Scottish waters; and over them there hung again the old torpedo fever. This reached a critical height after the *Royal Oak* was sent to the bottom in thirteen minutes by torpedoes from U47, and the *Barham* was torpedoed, within sight of the *Repulse*, shortly afterwards. There was little to distinguish the excursions as well as the alarums of twenty-two years before, from those experienced by the *Repulse* in 1939. Again there were North Sea sweeps, the abortive pursuit of reported German raiding forces in bitter northern waters. Only the occasional presence of an aircraft and the ever-present threat of German long-range bombers hinted at the coming revolution.

Among the *Repulse's* company in 1939 and 1940 there was an even greater sense of frustration than in 1917 and 1918. During the Norwegian campaign, when the small German navy succeeded in breaking through the British blockade to land invading forces on those neutral shores, she again failed to find an opportunity of using her guns.

When she was most needed off Norway and might have found good practice among German destroyers, she was dispatched to Iceland to meet sudden anxiety for the security of that strategically important island. A few rounds from her high-angle guns against German aircraft when she was docked at Rosyth, and a few seconds' action against Heinkels in the North Sea—mistaken until the last moment for RAF machines—was all the combat the *Repulse* was offered before she was earmarked for service in the Far East in August 1941. It had been hoped that she could be slightly modernised again before her departure. She was to have been fitted out with modern anti-aircraft radar—three sets each of 282 and 285—and fourteen of the latest Mk.16 4-inch high angle guns were to have been added in an American yard before she sailed to her new duties. But there was no time for any of this to be done. The political situation in the Far East was fast becoming critical and there was opportunity to mount only one more set of pom-poms before she sailed.

By the standards of her time, no criticism could be levelled at the *Prince of Wales*'s ability to deal with attacking aircraft, in any numbers. Against high level aircraft and low level attack at long range she could fire sixteen new 5.25-inch guns, at the rate of eighteen rounds per minute from each gun, to a range of 22,500 yards. To deal with intermediate and close air attack there were sixty-four two-pounder pom-poms, grouped in eights, supported by a bristling multitude of 40 millimetre Bofors, 20 millimetre Oerlikons and light machine-guns. There was steel up to six inches thick on her decks, and bulkheading of remarkable intricacy and ingenuity replaced the anti-torpedo "bulge" of earlier years. A third of her displacement weight was devoted to protective plating of one kind or another. Indestructibility under any combination of circumstances was the designer's aim, as it was the intention of those responsible for the design of all the last generation of battleships, such as the American *Washington*, Japanese *Yamato* and German *Tirpitz*. "Unsinkable" was not a term officially applied to the *Prince of Wales*; but it was in widespread use to describe her class, as so often before, in order to confound Britain's enemies and reassure herself and her friends.

It was in the offensive power of the *Prince of Wales* rather than in her powers of defence that she was always suspect. Her 14-inch guns were the smallest bore main weapons to be fitted to a British capital ship since the battle cruiser *Tiger* had been laid down in 1912. Fisher would have launched himself into ardent vituperation over this retrograde decision had he still been alive. It was claimed in their defence that the higher muzzle velocity and rate of fire (two rounds per minute) more than compensated for the lighter shell; that, like all its predecessors, its destructive power far exceeded that of any other naval gun in the world, and no less than twelve instead of eight or nine heavier guns, were to be carried. In fact, the Admiralty was neatly tricked into the 14-inch gun by the Americans and Japanese, and would clearly have preferred the heavier weapon. Japan had refused to sign the 1935 Naval Treaty which restricted the calibre of future naval guns to fourteen inches, but America agreed not to commit herself to larger guns until December 1935 in the hope that the Japanese Navy

Department would after all fall into line. In the absence of this reassurance, the first of the *Washington* class battleships, intended to carry 16-inch main armament, was laid down in 1937. It was clear that the United States Navy Department, in order to put the design and manufacture of the guns and their mountings in hand in time, had anticipated Japan's refusal by at least twelve months. But the Admiralty prepared in good faith for the fourteen inch restriction, and had proceeded past the point of no return—and the country to the brink of war—before awakening to the fact that our new battleships would carry the smallest-calibre guns of any in the world. (Not until later was it discovered that the Japanese guns were 18.1 inch.) Even the advantage of numbers of heavy guns for the *Prince of Wales* was lost when two had to be sacrificed to provide for heavier protection over the magazines.

The *Prince of Wales*'s 14-inch guns were put to severe trial within weeks of her joining the fleet, and with dockyard workmen still dissatisfied with the operation of the turrets, and still on board for further proving trials. The occasion was the breaking-out of the *Bismarck* in May 1941, and it was the *Prince of Wales*'s misfortune to be placed in company with an obsolete battle cruiser (the *Hood*) and so disposed in the brief running fight with the German battleship that only her forward turrets could be brought to bear on the target. One of her big guns remained inoperable for the course of the action, while all the turrets and guns were beset by breakdowns of one kind or another: a common state of affairs with new equipment on a new ship, but especially dangerous with an inexperienced crew under circumstances that became intolerable after the blowing up of the *Hood* and the concentration of both German vessels' fire on the *Prince of Wales*. She took severe punishment before she turned away. But those controversial guns, and the millions that had been spent on the ship herself, were justified by the three hits she made on the *Bismarck*. In the extraordinary series of chances and mischances that marked the long drawn-out hunting of the *Bismarck* several can be claimed as crucial in their contribution to her final destruction. One of these was the *Prince of Wales*'s shell hit in the German ship's bows, which severed an oil pipe, thus causing her to mark her trail like that of a wounded animal, and reduce her speed by two or three knots. It also prompted her captain to abandon the raid against Atlantic shipping, the main motive behind the break-out, and later helped to make possible Admiral Tovey's interception and final destruction of the battleship.

Withdrawn from the *Bismarck* pursuit through lack of fuel, the *Prince of Wales* paused on her homeward journey to Rosyth only to leave her wounded in Iceland and to bury her dead at sea. Her damage was spectacular but superficial, in part because of the high proportion of "duds" among the German 15-inch and 8-inch shells, and she was ready for sea again within a few weeks. Captain John Leach, who had been slightly wounded during the *Bismarck* engagement and had spent his leave in hospital, returned to his ship with the intention of "working-up" her company, that procedure to familiarise them with their equipment and duties which is especially important when a new class of big ship, manned by a high proportion of "hostilities only" men, is first commissioned. There had been no opportunity before the *Bismarck* action; but neither was there to be opportunity before her next action. As soon as she was ready for sea again, the *Prince of Wales* sailed for Scapa Flow, now considered safe from U-boat attack, and there, on the dour, drizzling morning of 4 August, 1941, received on board from a destroyer the Prime Minster, Winston Churchill, and his large staff. Harry Hopkins, President Roosevelt's roving ambassador, "returned dead-beat from Russia" according to Churchill, was also on board, to join in the talks in Newfoundland that had recently been suggested by the President.

There are several possible reasons for the choice of the *Prince of Wales* as conveyance for the Prime Minister to the Atlantic Conference. As she was still not "worked-up" to her full state of fighting efficiency, she may have been considered as less valuable a heavy unit to the battle fleet than any other capital ship. It may well have been thought, too, that her selection for this privileged rôle would raise the morale of her company, which was certainly not the highest in the fleet after her defeat by the *Bismarck*, her withdrawal from the battle, and the apparent failure of her gunnery and her guns. On the other hand, as one of the largest and newest class of battleship in the Royal Navy, she was most likely to impress by her presence the leader and aides of the most powerful neutral nation in the world. It would clearly have been unseemly for Winston Churchill to have arrived in Newfoundland in an aeroplane or passenger liner to meet the President. It was, however, eminently appropriate to steam into Placentia Bay in a 35,000 ton battleship, scarred by the rigours of war but disdainful of German bombers and U-boats alike (for much of her journey she had lacked even a destroyer escort), to parley with the leader of the world's second maritime power, who was using only a ten-year-old 9,000 ton cruiser for the occasion. The situation was in accord with the Prime Minister's sense of propriety for these circumstances, and there can be no doubt that he was largely instrumental in bringing it about. He also chose for the joint Anglo-American Divine Service on the quarterdeck of the *Prince of Wales* the day after her arrival, the hymn " For Those in Peril on the Sea." "It was a great hour to live," he wrote of this stirring moment in history. "Nearly half those who sang were soon to die."[22]

Among the more important subjects discussed by the two leaders before the final drafting and signature of the Atlantic Charter, was Japan and the growing crisis in the Far East. In no way was the final fate of the *Prince of Wales* directly sealed by these discussions, as has sometimes been suggested; but from the Atlantic Conference there arose the disputes and decisions that led to the dispatch of a battle fleet to the Far East; and among these vessels was the *Prince of Wales*, still a new ship, still not yet fully worked-up for combat in the important rôle allotted to her.

6 *The Inviolable Fortress*

It was with real reluctance that Britain, after the First World War, had allowed the United States to persuade her that the new threat to the wealth, influence and communications of the western democracies was likely to come from Japan. That country had, after all, been at least a nominal ally against Germany, and in 1919 the Anglo-Japanese Alliance was still in force. But not only was there some cause for American disquiet at Japanese Imperial aims; there was also the strength of a powerful creditor nation behind the persuasion. "As we had to choose between Japanese and American friendship," Churchill has written, "I had no doubts what our course should be."[22] There was, indeed, no other course to be taken.

If real danger existed, then it was not enough to end the old alliance and watch from a distance the development of the Japanese-American battleship race for control of the Pacific Ocean. Britain had to have what in contemporary jargon is called "the independent deterrent." Protection had also to be prepared for Britain's colonies and dominions: the priceless riches of the Malay States and Burma, and even of India; the trade routes to Hong Kong and the China coast, to Singapore, Calcutta, to Australia and New Zealand, as well as for the millions of people of these countries.

Any defence system has to have a central base, and this was the first problem to be considered in 1919, even before the termination of the Anglo-Japanese alliance. Hong Kong had for many years been the source of British naval strength in the Far East, and the Crown Colony's harbour was perfectly suitable for this purpose while the main duties of the Royal Navy were to maintain British interests in China, and the only likely trouble was from pirate junks. Ten years earlier, and of course in secret, the Committee of Imperial Defence had underlined the importance of rein-forcing Hong Kong if at any future time relations became strained between Japan and Britain. But if Japan, the world's third naval power, was to be considered as the future enemy, then Hong Kong was poorly situated strategically. When the CID considered the Eastern defence position again in 1921, the advantages of both Sydney and Singapore were considered. In the course of a visit to the Far East in 1919 in the battle cruiser *New Zealand*, Jellicoe had recommended that Sydney should form the main base, with Singapore as an advance base. Singapore, on the other hand, was one of the "five strategic keys" that "lock up the world"[23] as Marder has described it. The CID decided against Jellicoe's advice, and on 16 June, 1921, the Cabinet approved their recommendation that Singapore should be the main base against possible future Japanese aggression.

The British base at Singapore has been described as "an object of recurrent political controversy."[24] For the twenty years of its construction between the wars, the expenditure lavished on it was used to support Governments' alertness to Britain's defence needs, and to justify oppositions' cries of "extravagance!" It could be described as a bastion of Imperial defence, formidable and even impregnable; or as a piece of war-mongering folly—according to the side you were on. One Government might accelerate the defence work, another put a halt to it altogether. And when money was spent, of course it was well spent; when it was saved, it was equally admirable economy. The Singapore base's only consistent feature, to politicians, the British people, Britain's allies, and the harassed contractors and service chiefs, was that it was never for long out of the news.

It was not only in the interest of politicians to keep the Singapore base in the news. It was also in the interest of service departments, anxious for their status and their next estimates. For in Singapore's fortress and base can be seen, in concrete form and with great gun muzzles projecting from hidden cupolas, an Eastern reflection of the air versus sea power controversy of the 1920s and 1930s. At the beginning the function of the base was to act as a fortress with sufficient defensive strength to hold off any enemy long enough to allow the main fleet to arrive from home waters or the Mediterranean. It was considered unnecessary and undesirable for the battle fleet to be stationed out East permanently. Provisioning and maintenance would be complicated and expensive. The ships themselves deteriorated more quickly in the heat and humidity, and the climate was unhealthy for the men. Seventy days was the time to be taken for the main fleet to arrive; or so the CID was advised by the Board of Admiralty.

It would have been surprising if, at this time, when Trenchard and his allies were struggling for the survival and independence of the RAF, the premise that Britain's

Eastern defence was to be based primarily on sea power should have remained unquestioned. In fact, Singapore was to become as much a centre of inter-service as of political controversy. The far-sighted Jellicoe had, as early as 1919, not only preferred Sydney to Singapore, but had envisaged Britain's eastern defences built up on the joint foundations of air and sea power. At a time before any navy had commissioned an effective aircraft carrier, and torpedo-carrying aircraft were still in a primitive stage, he proposed a fleet made up of four carriers with torpedo bombers, supported by sixteen capital ships, cruisers, destroyers, submarines and auxiliary craft. Advanced air patrols were to be flown through Timor to Fiji. This was the view of Jellicoe, who also "expected aircraft in future wars to attack through clouds, using radio aids, with two- or three-ton bombs, or even larger."[25] Other admirals, and airmen, expounded their own views, characteristically and predictably. Beatty saw the defence of Singapore in the safe hands of a reduced version of the Grand Fleet he had so recently and ably commanded, and he was driven almost to distraction by the long running battle with Trenchard over the means to be employed in its defence. "That infernal place's name," he once wrote in despair to Lady Beatty, "will be engraved on my heart." Percy Scott stated in *The Times* (21 July, 1923), that "everyone ought to realise that our base at Singapore should be defended by submarines and aeroplanes, which would keep any battleships from coming within five hundred miles of the Island, as the Germans kept our battleships from coming near their coast." Trenchard, too, pleaded for a defence system based on air power, supported by submarines, mines and fixed batteries of medium artillery in place of the 15-inch weapons suggested by the Admiralty. A nucleus force of fighters, bombers, reconnaissance, and torpedo carrying machines would, in times of strained relations, be rapidly reinforced from Rangoon, India and Iraq, all part of his world-wide network of Imperial defence by air power.

After work on the base had been halted by the first Labour Government in 1924, as a contribution to world disarmament, the succeeding Conservative Cabinet decided that it was time a Sub-Committee of the Imperial Defence Committee, always a favourite refuge for harassed politicians, should settle the matter. Under the chairmanship of Lord Curzon, this committee finally recommended that heavy naval ordnance fixed in indestructible sites and supported by modest numbers of aircraft, should form the line of temporary defence pending the arrival of the main fleet. An airfield and seaplane base were to be built at Seletar. The Malayan jungle was considered to be sufficient defence against land attack.

Through all the delays and accelerations, the alarms and false alarms, the commendations and detractions, suffered by the Singapore base over the next thirteen years, the big gun maintained its predominant position: 15-inch guns firing out to sea from the island until more could be brought to bear with the arrival of the main fleet. Another committee, under Baldwin, confirmed this in December 1931. The power of the aeroplane was still unproven and unreliable. The fleet would come, in seventy days.

No threats existed in Europe at that time to endanger this arrangement, which became a basic tenet of British defence policy, on which the Dominions of Australia and

New Zealand depended for their security. Doubts about this assumption might have come earlier had they not been so politically dangerous. At least by 1937 the exposure of Fascist aims in Europe and the growth of the German and Italian navies must have brought into question the willingness of the Admiralty to send the main fleet to Singapore if the third member of the Axis joined the two European members in a war. But it was not until February 1939 that any kind of admission or reservation was made, in a Chiefs of Staff appreciation which said that "it is not possible to state definitely how soon after Japanese intervention a fleet could be dispatched to the Far East." The promise of a "main fleet" disappeared as suddenly as the period it would take to arrive. "Neither is it possible," went on the appreciation, "to enumerate precisely the size of the fleet that we could afford to send." This statement raised understandable alarm in Australia, where the Prime Minister asked for a closer definition than this of the timing and size of the relief force on which his country's safety might depend. The reply was scarcely reassuring. The size of the fleet would depend on when Japan entered the war and on what losses the Royal Navy suffered to that time, but commitments in Home, Atlantic and Mediterranean waters would be unlikely to allow for more than two capital ships. Then, in July 1939, the Committee of Imperial Defence decided that a safer lapse of time to allow for this "main fleet" to reach Singapore would be ninety rather than seventy days, a period that was shortly afterwards raised to one hundred and eighty days.

In the two years from the autumn of 1939 to the disasters

in Malaya, in the appeals and disputes, the frenzied efforts to stave off disaster and the contrasting lethargy and complacency, can be seen the microcosm of any distant outpost in crisis. The guilt and shame, the accusations and heart-searchings, that for more than twenty years followed this greatest disaster in British military history, have sometimes suggested that the English settlers and officials were a special breed of selfish and cowardly opportunists; that the servicemen and their commanders shamefully lacked the vigour and skill of, say, those who fought in the desert or Normandy. Those are scarcely acceptable conclusions. The rubber planters and infantrymen were no more different from other Englishmen than the heavy rescue volunteers of the London blitz and the paratroopers of Arnhem. Only in the moral and material circumstances imposed on them can any contrast be seen. Certainly, the military leaders quarrelled among themselves over how best to use their meagre equipment and supplies, and still misused them. It was true that the civil population was more concerned with running their estates than with the threat of invasion. But it should also be remembered that on the occasions when the defence of Malaya was given consideration in London, the result was contradiction and confusion, and that the rubber planters and other producers were constantly being reminded that their contribution to the war effort must be to step up their production to higher and higher levels. The real villain was the allegedly impregnable fortress, as disastrous a chimera to the Malay States as was the Maginot Line to France. Why should not the people of Singapore feel secure behind their five 15-inch big guns when on countless occasions they had been told on the best authority that they were secure? And why should not the military feel equally certain that they could never be overwhelmed? The dispatch of such small quantities of second class *matériel* alone suggested that the war leaders at home had the fullest confidence in their ability to hold off any Japanese attack. Not that such an attack was likely, they were told. From the Prime Minister down, the opinion in 1940 was that Japan, already fully occupied with a full-scale war against China, would never be so rash as to commit herself against the full might of America and Britain in the Pacific and South-East Asia.

Before 1940, Malaya's defence was the politicians' favourite whipping boy, the Singapore base a typical object of the fumbling opportunism of democracy at peace. After war broke out in Europe, Malaya became the victim of distance and the preoccupation of a parent with other distractions. There was no lack of these in 1941, to make the Far East more distant than ever before. The struggle in the Middle East was at a critical juncture. The army and the RAF had been sent to help the Greeks, and by the end of April had been withdrawn with grievous losses. A month later the bloody drama of the evacuation from Crete was being played out on the beaches of Sphakia. The situation in the desert after the heartening victories of the previous year had turned against us with the arrival of Rommel, who "had torn the new-won laurels from Wavell's brow and thrown them in the sand."[22] Wavell himself was relieved of his command. At sea, the monthly merchant shipping losses had risen to half a million tons, before the middle of the year, and with the sinking of the *Barham*, the *Ark Royal* and numerous destroyers and cruisers in the

Mediterranean, and the serious damage to three more capital ships as well as the loss of the *Hood*, our naval condition had reached its nadir. The invasion of Russia by Germany had transformed the overall strategical situation, but until winter closed in, the Russian armies continued to yield vast tracts of territory and caused only a drain on our meagre resources. The invasion threat still hung darkly over Britain, and on 10 May the Luftwaffe had proved that it was still able to set London on fire and kill or injure three thousand of its citizens without serious loss to itself. Everyone was saying a long, dour struggle lay ahead for the nation, and some responsible people were contemplating the possibility of stalemate and even of defeat.

With so many disasters and critical problems preying on him, it is scarcely to be wondered that Winston Churchill confessed that in his mind "the whole Japanese menace lay in a sinister twilight compared with our other needs." The order of priorities for all the likely theatres of war had been laid down by the Chiefs of Staff before the war. It had been drastically revised to meet the circumstances of 1941. Now, first came the defence of Britain against the ever-present danger of invasion and the slow strangling menace of the U-boat. Next the war in the Mediterranean and the Middle East. Thirdly the building up of supplies to Russia. And lastly the reinforcement of our strength in the Far East.

But it had not been possible completely to disregard the need for land forces in Malaya since a disturbing and highly secretive appreciation had been received from the GOC there, Major-General W. G. S. Dobbie, as early as 1938. This turned upside down all the existing plans by stating that Singapore might be attacked through the jungle from the north as well as from air and sea. The jungle, in fact, was henceforth still to be considered as a barrier, but not an impenetrable barrier. When Major-General L. V. Bond took over from Dobbie in July 1939, the construction of strong points some thirty miles inside Johore to the north of the Island had already begun, and airfields were being built, under the most trying circumstances. Then it became known that not only might the main fleet take as long as six months to arrive to defend Singapore, but that it was unlikely to consist of more than two capital ships. Not only, therefore, was Singapore apparently vulnerable to land as well as to sea and air attack, but expected naval reinforcements would be little more than nominal. Faced with this extraordinary *volte face* in Far East defence policy, General Bond demanded a minimum of twenty-six battalions and 556 front-line aircraft to compensate. The trickle of reinforcements began in August 1940 when two battalions were transferred to Malaya from Shanghai. Four Indian brigades and some Australian troops arrived late in 1940 and early in the New Year. In August 1941 the new GOC, Lieutenant-General A. E. Percival, informed the War Office that his minimum demand was for forty-eight infantry battalions and two tank regiments. By December he had under his command thirty-three battalions, little heavy artillery, few anti-aircraft guns, and no tanks at all.

The air picture was a great deal more unsatisfactory. The Chiefs of Staff had described over 500 aircraft as "far beyond the bounds of practical possibility." Their estimate of likely Japanese air strength available for an invasion came to the precise-sounding figure of 713, and they considered that 336 modern British fighting machines would be an adequate number to gain and hold control of the air. By December 1941 the RAF had 141 serviceable aircraft in Malaya and Singapore. It possessed no heavy bombers, transport or dive bombing machines. The fighter force to maintain domination of the skies above Malaya and Singapore and the surrounding seas consisted of four squadrons of tubby, obsolescent Brewster Buffaloes. These had given constant trouble since their arrival from America, demanding twenty-seven modifications before being either safe or battle-worthy. They had originally been fitted with .5 calibre machine-guns. Not only had these proved unsatisfactory, but their weight reduced the plane's rate of climb and service ceiling to pitiable levels. Even when these weapons were replaced by lighter .303 machine-guns, the ammunition limited to 350 rounds, and the fuel to eighty-four gallons, they still took half an hour to climb to 25,000 feet. Their radio equipment was out-of-date and unreliable, their maximum speed at their best height only 270 mph. There were fifty-two more Buffaloes in reserve, but nearly half were unserviceable. Their pilots were mostly New Zealanders and Australians; they were eager and enthusiastic but had only recently completed their training. They had had no combat experience, and the most potent aircraft they had previously flown were Hawker Harts, biplanes with fixed undercarriages.

It is not necessary to enter deeply into the courses followed by Japanese foreign policy, and the influences that affected it, from the Washington Treaty of 1921 to the moment of

H.M.S. Sultan, 1871. A representative of the era of compromise between sail and steam. She was commissioned before the torpedo became a serious threat, although in her later years thirty-five anti-torpedo boat guns were fitted

THE VICTORIAN BATTLESHIP

Eight years later: the sails have gone, there are just four massive 12.5 inch guns, and one-third of the weight is devoted to iron armour plate. H.M.S. Dreadnought's active life spanned the last quarter of the 19th century, the era of the battleship's total supremacy

BOMBER VERSUS BATTLESHIP

A direct hit by an aerial bomb during the bombing trials
off Chesapeake Bay in 1921

Vice-Admiral Sir David Beatty as C.-in-C. of the British Grand Fleet

Admiral of the Fleet Sir Dudley Pound, First Sea Lord in 1941

Above, H.M.S. Repulse; *below*, H.M.S. Prince of Wales

Admiral Sir Tom Phillips (right) and his Chief of Staff
Rear-Admiral Palliser, at Singapore, December 1941

Repulse and Prince of Wales (left) and a destroyer taking
evasive action during the first phase

A JAPANESE VIEW OF THE ATTACK

The first bombing attack, with Repulse (left) taking a hit
amidships

Prince of Wales with a heavy list and with some of her
company climbing down the starboard side. A photograph
taken from the bridge of the destroyer Express

Captain Tennant (left) of Repulse with his ship's Chaplain
shortly after they were picked out of the water

decision for war in Tokyo twenty years later. Since that nation's exposure to the modern world in the middle of the nineteenth century, the forces of moderation had carried strong weight, but had always been forced to yield when foreign actions could be shown to be humiliating or hostile, or when the country's most reasonable ambitions were frustrated. Between the wars, the tides of power ran steadily between the more liberal elements, represented by many of the commercial, industrial and intellectual classes among the civil population and the navy on the one hand, and the power of the army on the other. The army's strength and influence were increased by the ending of the alliance of friendship with Britain, the further frustration of Japanese designs on China with the Nine-Power Treaty, which followed the signature of the Washington Naval Treaty and guaranteed the integrity of that country, and perhaps most important of all, by America's anti-Asian Immigration laws, which deeply offended against the pride of the whole Japanese nation. All these acts were stored for fuel for the motionless but powerful machinery of Japanese militarism.

Throughout the First World War the Japanese Army, Prussian-trained and inspired with mystical dreams of world conquest, had sympathised with the German cause. With the Armistice, they therefore lost face and credit. They were content to hold back, for they knew that time was on their side. German influence in the Far East was dead, France was exhausted, British naval power reduced to a mere shadow of its former greatness and quite incapable of meeting simultaneously its commitments in Home Waters, the Mediterranean, the Far East, and of protecting its maritime links all over the world. Waves of benign pacifism seemed to wash against every shore. Only America demonstrated a positive unfriendliness and suspicion; and, in Japanese Army eyes, that nation, rich with the fruits of war and the millions owed to her by the old corrupt European imperialists, appeared set on a decade of total self-indulgence.

The militant extremist groups in Japan saw in the economic slump of 1929-30 the first sign of the tide turning in their favour. Japanese trade, already severely handicapped by discriminatory tariffs and barriers against her cheap goods, suffered serious losses, and considerable civil hardship followed. A carefully engineered bomb incident on the Southern Manchuria Railway led to Japanese and Chinese troops coming into conflict; and later, deaf to the protests of the League of Nations, Japan occupied the whole of Manchuria.

The preoccupation of the great European powers with their own crises and eruptions of dictatorships during the 1930s, helped to bring into office in 1936 the militarist Hirota Government. In the following year, on 7 July, another contrived incident near Peking led to major hostilities, which spread to south China ten months later. The China war rapidly spread and Japan made clear her intention of eventually ousting the last vestiges of Western influence by staging humiliating incidents against British and American citizens on Chinese soil. The crises and alarms following these incidents would have been greater, and the incidents themselves would have appeared less trifling, had there not been occurring more serious outrages in Europe. The Spanish Civil War and the earlier Abyssinian War, the aggressions against Austria, Albania and Czechoslovakia, were again conditioning the world to international violence.

As in all her earlier wars against China and Russia, Japan was dependent on outside aid for the means to keep her armed forces fighting against Chiang-Kai-Shek's Central Chinese Government. For three years her Army, Navy and Air Forces fought with American and Dutch oil, and the raw materials for their arms came largely from American mines, scrapyards and steel foundries. It was a highly profitable trade, and it was with a measure of reluctance and against the opposition of business interests, that the United States Government, in July 1939, finally gave six months' notice of the termination of the Japanese-American Commercial Treaty of 1911. Trading relations had been opened under the pressure of Commodore Perry in 1853. Eighty-six years later the U.S.A. found it necessary to close them again, completing the cycle; only the powerful American oil lobby helped to prevent the inclusion of that vital commodity, and the embargoes on other war materials did not become effective until the summer of 1940, but the political effect of this discrimination was at once felt in Japan. Simultaneously with this proof of the hostile intentions of democratic America, the militarist cliques could point to the dramatic failure of democracy in Europe, where France, Belgium and Holland had surrendered and Britain had become a beleaguered island, ripe for the taking. On 16 July, 1940, the army forced the resignation of the Yonai Government, and in its place was formed the Konoye Cabinet, with the violently anti-American Matsuoka as Foreign Minister and Tojo as Army Minister. Political parties were suppressed at home, and abroad the war against

China was pursued more vigorously, while pressure was put on the Dutch to step up their supply of raw materials, on the French Pétain Government to yield airfields in Indo-China to Japanese armed forces, and on Britain to close the Burma Road, which had for long been Chiang-Kai-Shek's chief supply route. In no case was there room for much argument. The Dutch agreed "to meet any reasonable demands for the raw materials specified"; the French opened their airfields to the Japanese Air Force; and the British Government, after failing to obtain any assurance of support from Washington, had also to give way and close the Burma Road.

The problem facing the United States in the winter of 1940-41 was not unlike the dilemma of Chamberlain's Government in Britain twenty-seven months earlier. The conclusion of a formal treaty by Japan with the victorious European Fascist dictatorships, the energetic prosecution of the China war, and the formation of the Eastern Asia Co-Prosperity Sphere with its clear threats against the vast riches of Siam, Malaya, Borneo and the Dutch islands; all these acts led to the conclusion that eventual war between the United States and Japan was inevitable. But as in Britain in 1938, the American people were not yet reconciled to the inevitability of military conflict, and the Chiefs of Staff were conscious of the need for more time to complete their preparations. Some sort of Munich-like interregnum was necessary, the length of which could be judged with some accuracy from the date when the United States cut off Japan's oil supplies, and that country's reserves reached the minimum level for the prosecution of a war that would, with the invasion of the Dutch East Indies' fields,

quickly yield her all the oil her armed forces would need in
the future. There was, of course, in the early weeks of 1941,
no mathematical certainty about the date when hostilities
would break out in the Pacific, for timing by oil barrels
was somewhat haphazard. But by calculating Japanese
consumption in relation to her gross bulk storage capacity
of sixty million barrels, and her domestic output of no more
than ten per cent of her requirements, it did at that time
appear likely that America had a maximum of twelve
months in which to prepare herself for war.

In April 1941 Japan secured the northern frontiers of her
empire by concluding a neutrality pact with Soviet Russia.
In July, Japanese troops marched into Indo-China in
strength to take up their positions for the drive south to
Malaya and Siam. The United States and Britain replied
by freezing Japanese assets, which meant not only the
cessation of all American oil supplies (eighty per cent of
Japanese consumption) but the virtual termination of
Japanese world trade. The threat of violence in the 1850s
had forced Japan to enter into the world of commerce and
trade; and less than one hundred years later she was thus
forcibly cut off from all further trading by a conflict of
interests with the nations that had winkled her from her
seclusion. But the ironies of the situation, and much else
besides, were lost in the diplomatic face-savings and
manœuvrings of the next six months, while the United
States increased its strength in the Pacific, and Admiral
Yamamoto completed his plans for his attack on the U.S.
Navy's base at Pearl Harbor. Time was on the side of
the United States, which, after July, could calculate the
daily consumption of oil barrels and vital raw materials

drawn from Japan's strategic reserves, and contemplate with satisfaction the weakening of Japan's economic position.

On 16 October, 1941, Prince Konoye, who still refused to recognise the inevitability of war with the United States, resigned in favour of Tojo himself. Both Governments were now irretrievably committed to conflict. Only two forlorn diplomatic gestures remained to be made. Following an Imperial Conference held on 5 November, the Japanese presented plans to Washington which offered a temporary *modus vivendi* with the understanding that neither country would "make an armed advance into any of the regions in the South-Eastern Asia and Southern Pacific areas excepting the part of French Indo-China where the Japanese troops are stationed at present," that the United States would not interfere with Japan's efforts to bring about "a restoration of general peace between Japan and China," and would restore normal commercial relations and the "required quantity of oil." Peace envoys were sent to Washington with the avowed intention of bringing about a *rapprochement*, only to be faced with a counter proposal from the American State Department which, among other demands, called for the withdrawal of all Japanese forces from China and Indo-China and the acceptance of Chiang-Kai-Shek's Government in Chungking. If, as Churchill described it, the oil embargo was a "stranglehold" that left the Japanese no alternative but war or agreement with the United States, then the State Department's "Ten-Point Note" of 26 November ruled out all hope of such agreement. For it was far beyond the bounds of reason that Japan would at this stage, and after some forty-five years of struggle through peace and war to enlarge her interests on the Asiatic mainland, surrender all her Chinese territorial conquests.

It was not only a matter of loss of face; the extremist elements had been allowed to gain undisputed control over the nation and had already settled for war simultaneously against Britain and the United States; a swift, crushing attack to gain total control of the Pacific, the riches of the East Indies, Malaya, Burma, Siam and India, and then a peace settlement negotiated from a position of overwhelming strength. This was the nature and scope of Japanese ambition, which, if fulfilled, would make her the most powerful nation in the world.

By 2 December the last details had been settled. The greatest carrier-borne strike force of aircraft in the world had already sailed from a lonely, ice-bound island in the Kuriles, steaming south-east across the Pacific, escorted by battleships, heavy cruisers and flotillas of destroyers. At dawn in five days' time the 360 bombers, torpedo planes and fighters would take off on their 275-miles' flight to Pearl Harbor; and the most decisive, the least costly, and the most strategically inept victory in the history of maritime warfare. Already the three Japanese divisions on the Chinese mainland had their marching orders for the attack on Hong Kong. General Homma's plans for the invasion of the Philippines with his 14th Army, supported by Vice-Admiral Tsukhara's 21st and 23rd Air Flotillas, were complete to the last detail. Far to the south-west, units of General Yamashita's 25th Army were embarked in their transports for the short sea voyage across the South China Sea to the east coast of Malaya, while others were detailed to march overland into Bangkok. The seaborne invasion was to be covered by battleships, cruisers and destroyers. Air support was provided by the 3rd Air Division comprising some 350 fighter, bomber and reconnaissance machines. In addition, there was based on airfields near Saigon in Indo-China, a great force of torpedo planes and bombers of the Japanese crack 22nd Air Flotilla. Their primary target was two British capital ships, already known to be steaming at best speed across the Indian Ocean.

As the danger to Malaya had heightened, as the threat to the riches of South-East Asia had become so great that it could no longer be disregarded, one more fundamental change had been made in British defence policy. The fleet, after all, was to come to Singapore; and not seventy or 180 days after the attack on the fortress. The battle fleet was already hastening east in order to strike fear in the hearts of those who threatened the Empire, to deter them from their predatory designs by its presence, and by the menacing power of its mighty guns.

7 *Dispatch of the Deterrent*

THE DAY OF THE BATTLESHIP as an effective weapon in maritime warfare was drawing rapidly to a close. Two crucial decisions leading to the sinking of five capital ships in the waters of Pearl Harbor, and two more in the Gulf of Siam, were to settle at last the fate of this esteemed and noble man-of-war. The first of these, taken many years earlier in the Japanese Navy Department as a result of the vehement persuasion of Admiral Isoroku Yamamoto, resulted in the use of air power in preference to the battle fleet as the first striking force against the United States and British Navies. The second, taken in Whitehall, resulted in the dispatch of a battle fleet to Singapore instead of squadrons of modern aircraft, tanks and artillery.

In 1941 it was still perfectly possible to argue that the capital ship had justified itself in its first two years of war. Its status in the eyes of the Admiralty and the Defence Committee remained high. It could still wield tremendous influence. Like the submarine and the torpedo boat before it, the bomber's alarm had seemed to ring hollow in the light of battle experience.

During the earliest days of the war at sea both the RAF and the Luftwaffe had made determined attempts to damage opposing battleships, as if to justify in combat for the first time the passionately held belief of Trenchard and Goering

—and air power disciples the world over—that the bomber was supreme, over the sea as well as over the land. On the day war was declared, an RAF reconnaissance machine sighted units of the German Navy apparently leaving harbour. Fifty-four bombers were at once dispatched but failed to locate them. The following day fourteen heavy and fifteen medium bombers attacked with great gallantry German battleships and cruisers off Wilhelmshaven and the western entrance to the Kiel Canal. The battle cruisers *Gneisenau* and *Scharnhorst* remained unscathed. The pocket battleship *Admiral Scheer* was hit several times but none of the bombs exploded. The only damage was to the cruiser *Emden*, caused by a crippled aircraft crashing into her, and this was not serious. One third of the Blenheim bombers were shot down, and the expensive experiment of attacking naval units in their well-defended bases was not for the present repeated.

The Luftwaffe fared no better in its first attacks on the Royal Navy in similar circumstances when two squadrons of Junkers 88 bombers attacked units of the Home Fleet in the Firth of Forth. The single bomb that struck its target failed to explode and four of the aircraft were destroyed. On the following day the Junkers returned to Scapa Flow, with no more useful results, succeeding only in damaging the demilitarised hulk of Jellicoe's old flagship of the 1914-18 war, *Iron Duke*. The defences at both places were strengthened but the attacks were not repeated.

It was one thing for bombers to fly over a great distance to attack warships possessing the additional protection of shore-based fighters and anti-aircraft guns, but quite another proposition, it might be thought, for high-level and dive-bombers to carry out a sustained assault on capital ships at sea and beyond the range of shore-based fighters. On 26 September, 1939, battle cruisers, an aircraft carrier and attendant cruisers and destroyers of the Royal Navy were in the North Sea acting as cover for a smaller force escorting home a damaged submarine. This naval force could scarcely have been caught under more disadvantageous circumstances. The capital ships were less securely armoured and only a few years more recent in construction than the *Ostfriesland*. Their anti-aircraft protection was far below what was later considered necessary in the Pacific War. But even that "sitting duck," the aircraft carrier, so often abused by Trenchard, came through unscathed when heavily dive-bombed from 6000 feet. The battle cruisers, too, were quite unharmed. Equally unsatisfactory results attended a further Luftwaffe raid in which about one hundred bombs were dropped on cruisers lacking even the support of carrier-borne fighters.

There then followed a combat in which the glory of pure sea power, undisturbed by the intervention of either submarine or aircraft, found full expression. This was the Battle of the River Plate in December 1939. In the first phase the German pocket-battleship *Graf Spee* inflicted great damage on the inferior British cruisers, but with the threat of overwhelming British reinforcements, retired to the safety of the neutral port of Montevideo, subsequently scuttling herself. This engagement provided a close parallel to the Battles of Coronel and Falklands in November and December of 1914, and seemed to confirm to those who might still have doubts that the traditional conception of sea power was as valid as it had ever been. The effect on the minds of the Admiralty and the Defence Committee—and the British people—was profound. "A quarter of a century had passed, but the puzzle was the same," commented Churchill, on the problem of tracking down the *Spee*. And the occurrence of this strenuous gun duel and the publicity it attracted, encouraged the comfortable feeling that little had changed since the last war. The armies of Britain and France were again facing the Germans on the Western Front. Winston Churchill was again at the Admiralty, the Navy still commanding the seas and dealing with enemy surface raiders with the same efficiency as before. Contrary to all expectations no air attack had been made on London, and those against our fleet had been abortive. At sea the gun, after all, still counted, and we still possessed the most powerful navy in the world. The feeling of familiarity was not wholly unpleasant. As in everything else, Adolph Hitler appeared to be wrong when he had proclaimed that "the day of Britain's sea power was past," and that "aircraft and U-boats have turned surface fleets into the obsolete playthings of the wealthy democracies. They are no longer a serious weapon in decisive warfare," he had said.

At the Battle of the River Plate the ships were far beyond the range of land-based aircraft, and the nearest aircraft carrier was 2,500 miles distant. With the increase of tempo of hostilities in the spring and summer of 1940, the damage caused by bomb attack to surface vessels increased sharply. This was to be expected, especially against light naval units working close inshore in support of evacuations in Norway and off Dunkirk. The Admiralty had long ago accepted the probability of losses when operating under these circumstances without adequate air cover and within comfortable range of land-based bombers and fighters. The evacuations from Greece and Crete in the face of fierce and persistent bombing attacks against our light forces also resulted in the loss of three cruisers and six destroyers and severe damage to many more.

Yet right up to the end of 1941, bombing attacks against armoured battleships, no matter how heavy or how closely these were pressed home, failed to do more than slight damage. For example, over a period of four months, from the end of March to the end of July 1941, RAF bombers of Coastal and Bomber Commands flew 1,875 sorties and dropped some 2000 tons of bombs on the German battle cruisers *Scharnhorst* and *Gneisenau* which lay as stationary targets in Brest harbour. Nine bombs hit their targets, at the cost of thirty-four aircraft, some of which were also engaged in laying mines in the harbour approaches. Only superficial damage was done to "Salmon & Gluckstein," as the constant reiteration of their names in communiqués caused them to be amiably nicknamed, and they remained a constant threat to our Atlantic convoys until the following February. "It must be recognised," wrote Churchill to the Chief of Air Staff in April 1941, "that the inability of Bomber Command to hit the enemy (battle) cruisers in Brest constitutes a very definite failure of this arm."

In Japan quite other conclusions were reached on the challenge of air power to sea power in the first two years of war in European waters. The fact that the Navy Department had in an advanced stage of construction the two largest battleships in the world did not blind them to a different interpretation of the record of the big gun at sea since September 1939. Before Japan came into the Second World War, Admiral Yamamoto and his followers could point to the fact that of nine capital ships sunk, only three had been sent to the bottom by the big gun. Of these, the French *Bretagne* had gone down while trapped in its harbour in the unhappy carnage of Oran, and the *Bismarck* had been crippled by the air torpedo before heavy shellfire had raked her, and had needed more torpedoes for the *coup de grâce*. Only the old *Hood*, like her fellow battle cruisers at Jutland, had succumbed in a straight artillery duel. The *Graf Spee* sent herself to the bottom when nothing but suicide appeared to be left open to her. The end of all the others, German, British and Italian, had been brought about by the torpedo.

By 1941, then, the reassertion of the torpedo as the most destructive weapon in sea warfare was as clearly recognised by the Japanese Navy Department as was the continuing supremacy of the capital ship, when properly supported, by the British Admiralty. This was regarded as a satisfactory state of affairs in Tokyo, where there also existed complete confidence that the Imperial Navy possessed the most advanced torpedoes in the world. Development of torpedo carriers—the submarines, destroyer and torpedo plane—had been intensified during the 1930s, after the successful trials of the first oxygen-powered torpedoes and the earlier decision to rely on the torpedo as the first striking weapon against the American Battle Fleet, in order to redress the balance of big-gun power laid down by the Washington Treaty.

Japan's overall strategic plan was to establish strong forces among the Caroline, Gilbert and Marshall islands, from which torpedo attacks would be launched, by submarine, destroyer and planes, against the American Fleet when it moved west to oppose the main Japanese landings on the islands of South-East Asia and Malaya. Speed was the keynote of this gigantic offensive operation: speed in securing the attack bases among the islands to the south and south-east, speed in securing the riches—and especially the oil—of the East Indies without which the whole military machine would be halted; and speed in crushing the American Pacific Fleet before it could intervene. By 1941, the Japanese destroyer and submarine forces, with their oxygen-powered "long lance" torpedoes, were the most powerful in the world. But it was in their Mitsubishi torpedo planes— the "Nells" and the "Bettys"—that the margin of superiority over those of Britain and America was most marked. The development of very long range land-based naval aircraft had begun in Japan in 1932. In 1936 came the "Type 96," with a speed of some 240 mph, and able to carry 800 kg. bombs or torpedoes. These were the finest naval attack aircraft in the world at this time. The "I type" followed in 1938, with the maximum speed up to about 300 mph, and possessing a strong defensive armament, and a range of up to 650 nautical miles. While the British Fleet Air Arm was still operating the 100-knot Swordfish long after Japan's entry into the war, and dropping 18-inch torpedoes from heights of around eighteen feet, the Japanese Navy Mitsubishis in the late 1930s were dropping their 24-inch torpedoes (explosive charge 460 lbs.) from heights of up to 1000 feet at the aircraft's maximum speed. Details of these powerful aircraft and torpedoes never leaked out; it is doubtful if they would have been believed anyway.

The first duties of these long-range land-based machines were to fly from their bases among the Pacific islands and surprise, intercept and destroy the American fleet when it moved east to protect the Philippines and the East Indies, and to destroy British naval forces operating from Singapore. The correctness of this reliance on the powerful, land-based torpedo plane as her first weapon of attack seemed to be justified by the achievements of obsolete British torpedo planes in European waters. The lessons of the Swordfish were taken more to heart in Tokyo than they were in London, or in Washington or Berlin for that matter. Considering their small numbers, their antiquity, the unreliability, short range and inaccuracy of the Royal Navy's torpedoes, the Swordfish's record was remarkable.

Carrier-borne Swordfish torpedo planes had taken part in many of the 1940 campaigns at sea and had had minor successes in spite of numerous and frustrating faults with their weapons, which on many occasions ran too shallow or too deep, or failed to explode when a strike was made. No capital ship on either side was sunk by an airborne torpedo in the first twelve months of the war. But portents of the future of the torpedo plane when the right conditions prevailed, and its killing powers were appreciated, occurred on several occasions, notably in November 1940, in an operation which the C in C Mediterranean, Admiral Sir Andrew Cunningham, described as "probably unsurpassed" in its economy of force. The Fleet Air Arm pilots in the Mediterranean had for long been relishing the opportunity of attacking the Italian Battle Fleet in the Mar Grande at

Taranto, an almost completely circular and enclosed outer anchorage strongly defended by balloon barrages, torpedo nets and anti-aircraft guns. During the autumn of 1940 these pilots carried out an intensive training programme, practising take-offs and landings at night with heavy loads under difficult conditions, and navigating what were then considered long distances over water in their Swordfish. Reconnaissance in the days before the raid by long-range Glenn Martin Marylands from Malta revealed the exact dispositions of the Italian Battle Fleet, and on the night of 11-12 November, twenty-one Swordfish in two waves, comprising in all twelve torpedo planes, five dive bombers and four aircraft carrying flares and bombs, took off from the *Illustrious*. Such was the inadequate range of the Swordfish that, although they were airborne less than two hundred miles from their target, they had to carry auxiliary fifty-gallon fuel tanks for the round trip. The dive bombing was mainly ineffectual, but the torpedo planes, weaving in and out of the "flak" bursts and the balloons at their maximum speed of some 140 mph, came down almost to sea level and dropped their torpedoes at point-blank range by the light of the flares. Three of the Italian battleships were sunk at their moorings for the cost of two aircraft.

Three months later, when other units of the Italian Fleet were hastening homewards from one of their rare forays, this time unsuccessfully attempting to interfere with British troop movements to Greece, five torpedo planes from HMS *Formidable* caught the Italian squadron and hit and slowed the new Italian battleship *Vittorio Veneto*. Later, eight more Swordfish flew through "the concentrated gunfire of this massed array of warships" and halted the heavy cruiser *Pola*. That night, this ship, and two more heavy cruisers and two destroyers sent back to her aid, were all destroyed by surface vessels of Admiral Cunningham's fleet which had been unable to close the main force. Total British losses in this action off Cape Matapan were one Swordfish aircraft.

In these two actions, then, the Fleet Air Arm had caused the sinking of three battleships, three heavy cruisers and two destroyers, and the damaging of another battleship, for the loss of just three machines. It was a ridiculously small price to pay for the recovery of maritime supremacy in the Eastern Mediterranean.

Final confirmation of the flexibility, range and power possessed by carrier-based aircraft, even of the vintage of the Swordfish, was given in the most exciting pursuit and engagement of the war, that of the *Bismarck* in May 1941. In the closing stages, in wild, dusk-shrouded confusion and with the most accurate and formidable anti-aircraft fire bursting about them, one Swordfish crew succeeded in landing home a torpedo in the battleship's stern, damaging her propellers and her steering gear. It was this blow, according to the official naval historian, that "sealed her fate." The destruction of the *Bismarck* was a crucial and decisive combined action, and its results were incalculable. "The effect upon the Japanese," Winston Churchill joyously telegraphed President Roosevelt, "will be highly beneficial. I expect they are doing all their sums again." Doubtless the Prime Minister was right. And one of their calculations may well have been that had the Royal Navy begun the hunt with three or four modern fleet carriers possessing as up-to-date torpedo planes and torpedoes as those in their own fleet—even at the expense of some of the eight capital ships ranging the ocean in search of the *Bismarck*—the enemy might have been disposed of much earlier and with the expenditure of many fewer lives and much less anxiety. For without the Swordfish, the Japanese Navy calculated, the *Bismarck* would surely have made port.

The Admiralty could as legitimately claim that without the *Prince of Wales*, which had earlier damaged the battleship, the *Bismarck* would have made port. It depended on how you did your sums. But the grand total of experience with the battleship in the first two years of war, had seemed to justify the Admiralty's decision to build the *Prince of Wales* and her sister ships. In the minds of Winston Churchill and the joint Chiefs of Staff, the battleship was still a most potent instrument of destruction, and, as a representation of power as a deterrent, still unsurpassed.

When it became clear, in the early summer of 1941, that the dangers of attack in the Far East could no longer be disregarded, the nature of the reinforcements, and the priorities, had to be considered. Britain had at home ninety-nine squadrons of modern fighters, mainly engaged in self-asserting "sweeps" over enemy-occupied territory. None were to be sent to the Far East, although Churchill was at this time pressing for no less than twenty squadrons to be sent to Iraq and Syria. Heavy bomber production was running at the rate of some 5000 a year; there was not one in the Far East. There were 400 heavy tanks in the Western Desert alone, hundreds more were going to Russia, production (excluding large importations from the U.S.A.) was some 280 per month; but none were to be sent to Singapore or Malaya.

"Narrowly we scanned our resources,"[22] wrote Winston Churchill; but he found nothing we could afford to send—except a battle fleet. It was not simply that distance lent enchantment, even when the riches of the Eastern Empire were in jeopardy. Churchill was still obsessed by Rommel and the tide of battle in the Western Desert. The Army's failure to finish the campaign there, once and for all, only strengthened Churchill's determination to reverse, in the teeth of protests from the CIGS, Sir John Dill, the old and long established priority in favour of the Far East needs over those of the Middle East.

There was, on the other hand, no dispute between Churchill and the Naval Staff over the need to dispatch naval reinforcements to the Far East. The only dispute here, and this was to develop later, was over the selection of the battle fleet and the timing of its arrival.

On 8 August, 1941, the Chiefs of Staff instructed the Joint Planning Staff to consider the whole question of reinforcements for the Far East, especially in terms of capital ships. This was done in anticipation of the outcome of the Atlantic Conference, then proceeding in Newfoundland. Four days later, Churchill sent a telegram to the Foreign Secretary, Anthony Eden, which summarised the discussion with Roosevelt over the Japanese situation and emphasised that the United States was hoping to gain time through negotiation in order that the Pacific and Far East defence position could be improved

The Naval Planning Staff were placed in a difficult position, because in fact no capital ships could be spared. In spite of the destruction of the *Bismarck*, it was considered that all the modern battleships, as they were completed, were still required in home waters to contain her sister ship, *Tirpitz*, in case she, too, determined to break out. The *Scharnhorst* and *Gneisenau* were still at Brest, a constant anxiety. The Mediterranean continued to demand battleship strength in spite of the mauling the Italian fleet had suffered, and its evident lack of spirit. Four capital ships out of a total force of fifteen were being refitted or having bomb damage attended to. However, as more new battleships reached the fleet and others returned from the dockyard, it would be possible, the Naval Staff considered, to build up a substantial Eastern Fleet. But it would take time. Four of the old "R" class battleships, which were unmodernised and had been under construction while Fisher was still at the Admiralty, could be sent to the Indian Ocean the following month, and this nucleus force increased to the extent of three more capital ships, an aircraft carrier, ten cruisers and other supporting craft by February 1942. The Admiralty made clear that this was intended as a force to protect trade in the Indian Ocean. It could not, on its own, hope to face the full might of the Japanese Navy; but, in conjunction with the powerful American Pacific Fleet, would provide a strong deterrent.

Churchill was back in London on 19 August, and the question of Far East reinforcements was the subject of his immediate inquiry. The Admiralty's plans were ready for him, and amid the hectic succession of meetings and discussions and the reports that accompanied his return, he found time to study them. He did not care for what he read.

In the mind of Winston Churchill, the key figure in the destruction of the *Prince of Wales* and *Repulse*, can be seen the confusion of paradoxes that surrounded the battleship during the last half century of its life. Churchill grew to manhood at a time when the lustre of Britain's maritime invincibility was undimmed and only a handful of eccentrics were predicting the big gun's *commencement de la fin* as the ultimate weapon at sea. Much of his historical education, from his earliest days at school, was concerned with Britain's naval history, from the apocryphal tales of King Alfred to Southey's *Life of Nelson*. No orthodox schooling in Victorian times could escape this heavy weight of importance attached to Britain's naval heroes and maritime history. When in 1911 Churchill achieved his ambition by becoming First Lord, at the age of thirty-six, he had experienced at first hand only land warfare, mainly in South Africa. But he had since childhood been deeply interested in the roots and functions of naval power and had a wide knowledge of the administration, the ships and the men of the Royal Navy. Like so many of his countrymen, he was also strongly and emotionally conscious of the faith the British Empire confided in the battle fleet's power, and the near-religious source of security and well-being it provided in a mainly hostile and wholly inferior world. It is scarcely possible to over-emphasise the depths of emotion and satisfaction its beholders derived from the sight of the British Fleet—at, say, the immense Diamond Jubilee Review at Spithead in 1897. Winston Churchill embraced this national cult with ardour.

It is not until Churchill's first term of office at the Admiralty, from 1911 to 1915, that there can be discerned the first signs of the contradictions in his whole attitude to sea power, that must have sorely tried and confused him, and his supporters, in the years ahead. Within weeks of his arrival at the Admiralty, his alert, inquiring mind was beginning to question the basic tenets of his country's naval policy and to search out the value of new weapons. Although Fisher had recently been replaced by Sir Arthur Wilson as First Sea Lord, Fisher's guidance was still sought, and most willingly given, and his influence in Whitehall remained powerful. On Churchill it was profound. He may have been anxious about Fisher's volcanic intemperance, but he savoured with delight his disrespect for accepted creeds and suppositions, and his interest in new weapons. Fisher certainly transmitted to Churchill, for example, some of his own disquiet about the coming threat of air power. Already in 1912 Churchill was expressing his "great anxiety" about bombing attacks from airships, and stating his opinion that ships in harbour would be "absolutely defenceless against this form of attack." He gave enthusiastic support to the experiments with heavier- and lighter-than-air machines then going on at Farnborough and in the following year he approved of the construction of two rigid and six non-rigid airships. He even suggested that Britain should sell two pre-dreadnought battleships to Turkey for £100,000 apiece and buy airships with the money. His airship period was short-lived, however. Accidents at Farnborough and the obvious vulnerability of these inflammable gas-bags caused him to change his mind, and, in Fisher's words, "he went mad on aeroplanes."

Encouraged by Churchill, a nucleus force of seaplanes and aeroplanes for the Navy was built up during 1913 and 1914, ostensibly as a spotting and reconnaissance force. The Board of Admiralty was not much interested, and when seventeen seaplanes and two flights of aeroplanes swept low over the fleet when King George was reviewing it in July 1914, the reason for their altitude was, according to most officers present, their inability to go any higher.

The aeroplane was to Churchill only one among many possible weapons of the future that fleetingly held his attention and were engulfed both by his own preoccupation with multitudes of other ideas and experiments, and by the Board's severe conservatism. Even with the authority provided by his position as First Lord, single-minded and continuous pressure would have been needed in 1914 to cause any serious attention to be paid to the aeroplane as a possible future threat to the all-powerful battle fleet. Churchill was too busy harassing the Board with other schemes, and interfering with the normal functions of every branch of the service, to concentrate his fire and make such an impression. Besides, whatever doubts his intellect might throw up, his heart lay still with the Grand Fleet after war came in August. There is nothing like the firing of a big gun to confirm in men's minds its awful power and omnipotence. And the fierce and romantic naval contests—the successes at Heligoland Bight and Dogger Bank, the swift retribution at the Falklands for the Coronel tragedy—in the opening months of the war, all tended to confirm the traditional functions of sea power.

In Churchill's brief period as war-time First Lord, there is no evidence of the warring contradictions that later made his attitude towards the battleship so puzzling. But in the hurly-burly of war-time operations, in the rancorous disputes and bitterness that characterised the Admiralty during the winter of 1914-15, in the heartbreaking quarrel with Fisher over the Dardanelles, followed by the resignation of the First Sea Lord and the dismissal of Churchill himself, can be found the origins of another dispute twenty-six years later.

Churchill was the most trying and restless First Lord the Admiralty had ever known. He interfered constantly in the day-to-day duties of his subordinates, driving them to exasperation, and then to a point where so much responsibility was taken from them that they naturally felt that their obligations were proportionately reduced. He was overbearing, intolerant and intimidating. His opponents were many, his supporters few in those days. From many there was not even grudging respect. With fleet operations on a war basis, the feeling of disquiet about the First Lord's habitual interference grew rapidly. As Roskill has revealed,[26] evidence is now available to suggest strongly that, but for Churchill's meddling and the confusion of orders that arose from it, the German battle cruiser *Goeben* and the cruiser *Breslau* would never have escaped through the Mediterranean to Turkey, causing that country's entry into the war on the German side. He vetoed Fisher's decision over the movements of ships—from squadrons to individual vessels—and fretted constantly over every proposal, however great or small its apparent significance. He was always suspicious that opinions and decisions were being reached behind his back, that he might be outwitted or outmanoeuvred. Fisher and Jellicoe kept up a steady stream of correspondence during those opening months of war, and Fisher's letters show that Churchill was jealous of the intimacy of their professional relationship, which as a mere politician he could not hope to match. Fisher often pleaded with Jellicoe to write sometimes to Churchill, too, ("he is pining for a letter") if only for the sake of peace.

The strains of aggression and truculence, the determination to demonstrate superior intellectual and technical knowledge and experience to that of the professionals, the sense of isolation he experienced as only an honorary member of a tightly-knit, closed and tradition-bound club, all suggest that Churchill did not perhaps feel the self-confidence that has usually been ascribed to him. To be First Lord of the Admiralty at one of the most critical times in the Navy's history, marked for the young Minister a moment of destiny and supreme challenge. He claimed to have taken his political life in his hands when he persuaded the King and the Prime Minister to let him have Fisher as his First Sea Lord. In company with this renowned figure, he saw the fulfilment of his greatest ambition in the assertion of British maritime power and the crushing of the German Fleet. Early in 1915, with the success of the Dogger Bank redounding to their joint credit and the real hope of a massive meeting of the battle fleets in the North Sea (the submarine offensive had not then developed), realisation seemed near. Then everything crumbled in the unseemly wrangles over the Dardanelles campaign. Fisher, who, Churchill claimed, had promised "to stand by me and see me through" resigned in protest; and Churchill followed him into the wilderness. This event made a deep and enduring impact on the towering ambitions of a brilliant young man, and brought him political maturity at the price of bitter disappointment. It also produced another result that was to have delayed but profound effects. These reached their most critical state, and final catastrophe, in the naval events of autumn, 1941.

After 1915, Churchill was to be even more mistrustful than before of the motives and decisions of admirals. All his first hidden suspicions of their intellectual superiority had been shattered. They were, indeed, as short-sighted and little-gifted in the conduct of a maritime war as he had attempted to show them, and prove to himself, that they were. In the idle months of rumination that lay ahead, before at last a new Ministerial appointment came his way, Churchill had full opportunity to decide that, if ever control over the Admiralty came his way again, he would assert himself as boldly and ruthlessly as before. Admirals could be untrustworthy, incompetent and cunning.

The hard facts of political life, and simple opportunism, can account for the fluctuations of loyalty to the battle fleet of many politicians in Britain and America between the wars. Samuel Hoare, for example, was the most ardent advocate of air power, and, as has been told, made his first political reputation by leading the campaign to preserve the RAF and retain the Naval Air Arm under its control. Fifteen years later, as First Lord, he felt it his duty to press for the building of five new battleships and for winning back the Fleet Air Arm to the Admiralty. He was successful in both capacities. Churchill, now a mature politician, showed the same aptitude for switching his advocacy to the situation and occasion. P. R. C. Groves has written sharply of "the paradox of Winston Churchill" in his book *Behind the Smoke Screen*, contrasting his attitude when, as Secretary of State for Air in 1920, he endorsed and implemented the views of the Air Staff on the military mind's attitude to air power, while he "expressed the most scathing indictment of the same mentality" in his war memoirs. But such criticism is scarcely just, as the switching of loyalties must always be the prerogative of any parliamentary politician.

It is evident that the same contrary pressures preyed on Churchill's mind during the bomb-versus-battleship debates of the 1920s and 1930s as had influenced his judgment while he was at the Admiralty in 1911-1915. Deeply-rooted sentiment, the traditional values of sea power and the mystique of the big gun on the one hand, continued their conflict against his cooler powers of inquiry and his deep respect for the scientist. In Parliament or in public, when the occasion arose, he continued stoutly to defend the battleship, its power as a deterrent and its ability to defend itself against any form of attack. Both Beatty and Trenchard attacked him when, as Chancellor of the Exchequer, he had been obliged to cut away at their estimates; but it was Beatty who suffered least. When service economies ended at last in the mid-1930s, he publicly backed the creation of a modern battle fleet. He frequently quoted the somewhat doubtful lessons of the Spanish Civil War, in which modern sea and air weapons had been given a first opportunity of testing their strength. "The extravagant claims of a certain school of air experts have not been fulfilled," he claimed in an article in the *Daily Telegraph* on 1 September, 1938. "We were assured some time ago that navies were obsolete and that great battleships, costing seven or eight million pounds, would easily be destroyed by aeroplanes costing only a few thousands. . . . The Spanish fleets are not well equipped with anti-aircraft artillery. Their vessels are not well equipped with anti-aircraft artillery. Their vessels have no special armour against overhead attack. Yet we have seen them cruising about the coast, often in full view from the shore, apparently as free from danger as if aeroplanes had never been invented." Modern planes, manned largely by experienced Russian, German and Italian pilots, and flying from shore aerodromes fifteen minutes' flying time from highly prized naval vessels, had apparently made no attempt to attack. "Why are they not able to do it?" To Churchill, this showed "the limitations rather than the strength of the air weapon." So far as the Royal Navy was concerned, "it now looks as if the original danger was much exaggerated. . . . Our ships have received immense and formidable protection. . . . It would seem to follow, therefore, that all the implications of sea power based upon the possession of a superior line of battleships still retain their validity. If this be true, and it is the view both of the British and American naval authorities, the command of the seas would appear to rest unchallenged with either of the navies of Britain or the United States. This, added to the undoubted obsolescence of the submarine as a decisive war weapon, should give a feeling of confidence and security, so far as the seas and oceans are concerned, to the Western democracies."

At this time Britain was close to the brink of war with Germany, and the only branch of arms in which we possessed an overwhelming advantage was heavy warships.

Germany had no battle fleet to speak of. It was clearly not good politics or policy to show lack of confidence in the capital ship, especially as there were five new ones on the stocks. The circumstances had something in common with those of 1914. Besides, when a new war came, Churchill clearly hoped again for the Admiralty.

Some evidence leads to the view that Churchill had by this time already recognised that the days when Britain's maritime security rested finally with the battle fleet were past, while the battleship's ability to command respect and to deter still remained. For patriotic reasons alone he had to keep these views private. With privacy assured, however, he could be persuaded to express different views on the battle fleet. On 14 February, 1936, for example, at a dinner in a private room at Bucks, Churchill, Major-General Fuller, Lord Trenchard and Captain Liddell Hart, met, as guests of Alfred Duff-Cooper, to discuss defence problems. Liddell Hart kept notes at the time, and according to these, the nature and functions of the future fleet was one of the subjects. Trenchard, of course, complained of the continued dominating influence of the Admiralty in defence matters; then Churchill said that what was really wanted was more flotilla craft, but that "the laying down of one or two battleships would act as a sort of bluff." On the defence of Singapore, he preferred to put his faith in fixed artillery, in flotillas and aircraft rather than a battle fleet.

Five and a half years later, and with two years of maritime war experience to draw on, Winston Churchill's confidence in the battleship's power to bluff a potential enemy remained. The dispatch of a battle fleet to the Far

East might indeed be a decisive deterrent, he considered. But he disagreed with the Admiralty's proposed steady creation of a comparatively large force of older capital ships and supporting forces in the Indian Ocean. On 25 August, 1941, after his study of the Admiralty's plan, he sent to the First Lord, A. V. Alexander, and the First Sea Lord, Admiral Sir Dudley Pound, a memorandum proposing more urgent and dramatic steps. Drawing on the experience of the alarms aroused and the forces occupied by the threat of one or two fast and modern German battleships breaking out into the Atlantic, he pressed for "a formidable, fast, high-class squadron" consisting of one of the new battleships, a battle cruiser and aircraft carrier. This "would exert a paralysing effect on Japanese naval action," and act as a gesture of reassurance to New Zealand and Australia. The Dominion Governments would be advised early on of its proposed dispatch, and its passage and arrival in Singapore would be publicised to the world as a demonstration of our determination to halt any further southern advance of Japanese militarism.

Three days later, on 28 August, the Admiralty replied with a long memorandum* seeking again to justify their more cautious proposal to build up a balanced fleet in the Indian Ocean, while retaining the modern *Prince of Wales* and *King George V* in European waters. The justification for this arrangement was summed up thus:

"By sending capital ships to escort our convoys in the Indian Ocean we hope to deter the Japanese from sending any of their battleships to this area.

* This memorandum and earlier correspondence on the subject are reproduced in Churchill's *The Second World War*, iii, Appendix K.

"By sending a battle cruiser and aircraft carrier to the Indian Ocean we hope to deter the Japanese from sending their 8-inch gun cruisers to attack our trade in this area.

"It is not considered that the substitution of one of the *King George V* class for one of the above would give sufficient added security to justify the disadvantages which her absence from the home area would involve, as her speed is inadequate to run down a Japanese 8-inch gun cruiser.

"Depending on the situation at the time, and if war with Japan has not broken out, it may be found desirable to send *Nelson*, *Rodney*, *Renown* and the aircraft carrier to Singapore in the first instance, as they would thus form a greater deterrent. If war eventuated they would have to retire to Trincomalee."

Churchill replied at once that this was a faulty disposition. The judgment of Sir Dudley Pound and his staff he found inherently "unsound" on this question. The old "R" class battleships, which were to operate in the Indian Ocean on escort duties, he considered, would be "floating coffins." The retention in Home waters of both the new battleships to contain German attacks against our trade was "a serious reflection upon the design of our latest ships."

More urgent matters then intervened, and perhaps to the relief of the Admiralty Planning Staff, the matter was dropped. There is no record of any further discussion or action on the question of Eastern reinforcements throughout the month of September 1941, and it was not until mid-October that it was again raised. The fall of the Konoye Government in Japan was at this time giving the Foreign Office grave anxiety. The effect of the American embargoes was evidently encouraging the most extreme elements in Japan's political structure, and these gained further encouragement from Russian military defeats. On 16 October, Anthony Eden pointed out the dangers in a memorandum to Churchill, stressing the importance of sending deterrent forces urgently to the Far East. At a Defence Committee meeting the next day the opposing claims made seven weeks earlier were repeated by Churchill on the one hand and Alexander, for the Admiralty, on the other. The *impasse* appeared to be complete. But further weight was added to the Prime Minister's cause when Eden said that from the political point of view—for the purpose of reassuring the Australian and New Zealand Governments in particular—the dispatch of one modern battleship would be more valuable than any number of old capital ships.

It was not until 20 October that the Admiralty's resolution cracked under the continuing pressure of Churchill and Eden. At a Chiefs of Staff meeting, Dudley Pound for the last time argued that Churchill's proposed token force would not prevent Japan from invading Malaya, as the enemy could well afford to spare a force of capital ships capable of overwhelming one battleship and a battle cruiser, but that a more formidable squadron, though it might be more distant and composed of slower vessels, would oblige Japan to send south the greater part of their battle fleet "and thus uncover Japan" to the American Navy. Churchill countered this argument by stressing his belief that a direct attack against Malaya's coastline was most unlikely, and that a more serious threat was from swift Japanese trade-route raiding forces, against which slower battleships in the Indian Ocean would be helpless. Pound recognised the hopelessness of further argument and came forward with a compromise. The *Repulse* would already be in the Indian Ocean, having completed the escort of a Middle East convoy round the Cape. The *Prince of Wales*, he suggested, should go to Cape Town, from whence she could be recalled if urgently required in Home waters, and there her further movements would be decided. The new aircraft carrier, *Indomitable*, would join the *Prince of Wales* en route. Churchill agreed at once, and the Defence Committee accepted the First Sea Lord's compromise.

The loyalty of Admiral Sir Dudley Pound is unquestioned. Captain S. W. Roskill has written that "if a decision was taken against his advice and things went wrong, he never let it be known that he had tried to prevent the steps which ended in misfortune."[17] And this same authority has recently revealed publicly for the first time that in a letter to Churchill four months after the disaster, Pound insisted that the dispatch to the Far East of the *Prince of Wales* "was in accordance with my advice." Loyalty to one's superior could scarcely go further than this. No more diplomatic or understanding First Sea Lord and working partner for Churchill than Pound was available. The news of Churchill's return to the Admiralty had been received with grave anxiety by some senior officers who had experienced at first hand his arbitrariness and unpredictability in 1914-15. This anxiety must have been shared by Pound himself, who had been one of Fisher's staff officers before the May 1915 debacle. Referring to this moment of reacquaintance, Churchill has written of how they eyed one another "amicably if doubtfully"; and how "from the earliest days our friendship and mutual confidence grew and ripened."[27] It was not only that Churchill recognised the value of Pound's experience and the breadth of his vision. Pound's insistence on controlling tightly the movements and dispositions of the fleet, and even of individual vessels, and his reluctance to permit any sort of decentralisation of his authority, admirably suited Churchill. The affection and admiration were reciprocal. Indeed, in the early months of war, Pound was only too ready to fall in with the First Lord's more daring proposals. But by 1941 Pound had learnt how to steer Churchill subtly towards more pressing problems without in any way compromising his own sense of loyalty, or his admiration for the Prime Minister. The most effective method he discovered of managing Churchill was, where possible after the receipt of a "prayer," to allow a lapse of time which was filled with a multitude of other matters, and then quietly to bring to bear the considered opinions of the board. These were usually confirmed by the Chiefs of Staff; then reluctantly, and not always graciously, agreed to by Churchill himself. This had worked on a number of occasions, and Pound must have hoped that the six weeks from the end of August to mid-October 1941 would serve the same purpose when he presented the Admiralty's case for the last time at the Chiefs of Staff meeting on 20 October. But this time, two unpredictable factors worked against him. Churchill had the political support of Eden, who had insisted that the question of Eastern reinforcements was urgent and that a modern battleship must go; and Pound's own powers of resistance were weaker than they had been a year earlier.

By the late summer of 1941, Sir Dudley Pound was

already a sick man, and senior officers who were close to him have suggested that the rigours of his self-imposed standards, added to the demands made on him by the Prime Minister, had caused a weakening in the resolution of his defences against outside pressure, if not in his judgment. Although he was only sixty-four years old, his health had been affected by an old leg injury, which had led to osteo-arthritis in his left hip, a most painful disability. Sleep was difficult for him, and even the short periods he could some-times snatch were often spoiled by the call of duty, and especially by Churchill, whose odd sleeping hours brought so many of his subordinates near to despair. He often took short naps during conferences, and although it has been claimed for him that he still managed to keep abreast of the discussion, this has been disputed by others who were present on these occasions. Pound was further handicapped by his deafness, and it was Churchill's practice, accepted with resigned humour by those also present, to push through proposals, unlikely to please the First Sea Lord, either in a low tone or when he was asleep.

What has never been properly explained is why, after the Chiefs of Staff decision of 20 October that the *Prince of Wales* should proceed to Cape Town, the Admiralty informed all naval authorities the following day that the battleship would sail for Singapore. There is, apparently, no record, official and secret or public, that any written order was made to cause this vital change of destination, which directly opposed the compromise suggested by Pound and agreed to the preceding day. The issue is further confused by the fact that, first, both on 31 October and 5 November Churchill informed the Dominion

Premiers that in order to deter Japanese aggression the battleship had already sailed for the Indian Ocean to join the *Repulse* and form the nucleus of a battle fleet; and, second, that the Commander-in-Chief himself was never in any doubt that his eventual destination was Singapore. In addition, as Roskill confirms in his official history, when on 1 November Churchill "asked the First Sea Lord what his plans were if it was decided that she should go on to Singapore," Pound replied that he intended "to review the situation generally just before the *Prince of Wales* reaches Cape Town." "Good. Fix up the best plan meanwhile," replied Churchill. It would have been unusual for any far-reaching change of plan of this nature to have been made verbally, but the conclusion that Churchill pressed home his advantage on Pound, personally or by telephone, immediately after the Chiefs of Staff meeting on 20 October, cannot be ruled out.

The selection of the officer for the key rôle of Commander-in-Chief of the Eastern Fleet aroused no controversy, for the decision had long been made. He was Acting Admiral Sir Tom Phillips, a man of small stature and implacable will, whose asperity could intimidate even his seniors. He was known as "Tom Thumb" to the lower decks and among his fellow officers. He was fifty-three years old, with a pale countenance, sharp, close-set eyes and a down-turned mouth that suggested hidden kindliness and a total absence of humour. He was a good family man, and his hobby was repairing watches. He had few other interests outside the service. His health was not robust. Phillips had joined the Navy in 1903 and had received his training and gained his first promotion during the great Fisher era of British maritime supremacy. He did well, gaining first-class certificates, and specialised in navigation. His term in the *Britannia* produced six flag officers, and one of these to-day classes him as the most intelligent of them all. During the First World War he served in cruisers in the Mediterranean and the Far East, becoming an acting captain in 1918. Staff work and operational planning filled most of his years between the wars. After a Staff College course, he three times served on the planning staff. In 1925 he worked under Pound on the operational staff in the Mediterranean. A firm bond of affection and trust grew up between the two men and when Pound became First Sea Lord in 1939, there was no surprise when he selected Phillips as his Deputy Chief of Naval Staff. The First Lord, Alexander, considered him "a great leader, a great Christian, a man of perhaps as high a standard of conduct as it would be possible to find anywhere in any society." As DCNS, Phillips worked closely with Pound, and with Churchill, both when he was First Lord and later when he became Prime Minister, in the turbulent, demanding and always critical conditions that governed the activities in Plans and Operations at the Admiralty during the first two years of war. Churchill admired Phillips's self-assurance, his vision, his minute attention to detail, and the authority and knowledge that years of staff work had taught him. The two men had much in common, and shared the same offensive spirit in their planning. Phillips warmly backed Churchill's plan for forcing a passage into the Baltic in 1939, an operation that owed much to Fisher's inspiration. They worked together amicably on many other projects, some almost as extraordinary as "Operation Catherine." They recognised and respected one another's intolerance and impatience, capacity for work and unyielding nature. A warm friendship seems to have grown up between the First Lord and the Deputy Chief of Naval Staff, and in February 1940 Churchill recommended Phillips for the rank of Acting Vice-Admiral. When Churchill became Prime Minister, Phillips sometimes stayed at Chequers at week-ends.

A change in the relationship between the two men became apparent in the winter of 1940. They first fell out over differences of opinion on the value of strategic bombing. Phillips had small regard either for the strategic or tactical worth of the bomber aeroplane. In the years between the wars he had remained a firm big-gun man, and his confidence in the offensive and defensive powers of the capital ship was undiminished by the experiences of 1939 and 1940. Furthermore, it was his conviction that all warships at sea, if properly equipped with anti-aircraft armament and well-trained gun crews, could repel air attack, even from shore-based aircraft. This stemmed in part from the measures he had taken before the war when serving in destroyers. In 1936, he had witnessed the abortive attempts of the combined anti-aircraft fire of the Home Fleet to make any impression on a slow, steadily moving, radio-controlled target plane (a "Queen Bee"). This alarming exhibition had caused him to work out a set of complex evolutions for escorting destroyers to carry out in the event of air attack that would, assuming highly-skilled gun crews, ensure the protection of their escort and themselves. Phillips believed that the heavy high-angle gun, multiple pom-pom and machine-gun, in sufficient numbers and properly operated, represented the answer to any threat from the air.

The success of air attacks against warships off Norway and Greece, in particular, and of the torpedo planes against the Italian Fleet at Taranto, did not shake Phillips's confidence. Many of the ships sunk, he considered, had been caught isolated and at a disadvantage, rendering them incapable of co-ordinating and combining their defence, or had been defended with insufficient skill or vigour.

When the C in C of the Mediterranean Fleet complained of the impossibility of driving off determined air attacks on light naval forces operating in the coastal waters of Crete and Greece, Phillips expressed disbelief and complained of the unsatisfactory handling of the high-angle guns. In common with other senior naval officers, he praised and welcomed the Fleet Air Arm success at Taranto, but believed that a similar attack against a British base would have failed.

Neither was Phillips alone in his suspicion of the effectiveness of strategic bombing against land targets. Although it was on this very question that Phillips first antagonised the Prime Minister by his opposition, Churchill himself found it necessary at this time to warn the Chief of Air Staff against putting his claims too high. Quoting the exaggerated picture of air destruction before the war and Britain's own survival during 1940, he gave his opinion that "even if all the towns of Germany were rendered largely uninhabitable it does not follow that the military control would be weakened or even that war industry could not be carried on."[22] In the past, too, Churchill had often pointed to the absence of real damage and the hardening of civil morale as a result of bombing in the Spanish

Civil War. When the Chiefs of Staff decided on retaliatory bombing of German cities in the autumn of 1940, Phillips strongly opposed it. It was, he believed, a misuse of our slender resources. His opinions were disregarded, and a coolness in his relationship with Churchill became observable. The week-ends at Chequers ceased. But worse was to come.

Churchill is doubtless right in claiming the unanimity of the Chiefs of Staff and the War Cabinet in their decision to give military aid to Greece in March 1941. If Pound privately disagreed, there is no record of it. But Phillips, as Vice Chief of Naval Staff (the title had been changed), expressed disagreement forcefully and repeatedly. He prophesied waste and disaster. It was his opinion that our prime object was to reopen communications in the western Mediterranean and regain the maritime control we had lost to the German and Italian air forces. At the same time he strongly opposed Churchill's plan to establish long-range fighter airfields along the North African coast to provide air cover for convoys of R.N. ships.

The clash of powerful wills, that had once worked in sympathetic harmony, destroyed all confidence between these two self-assertive men. Churchill, recognising the same powers of resistance and misguided obstinacy which he had seen in Fisher in 1915, and which had resulted in political disaster for him then, determined to be rid of Tom Phillips as soon as he could without causing a crisis at the Admiralty. The opportunity to do so was not long delayed. Phillips had been one of the strongest advocates of a Far Eastern Fleet, and the reinforcement of Malaya to meet the challenge of Japan, which he took more seriously than many of those at least as qualified as he was to recognise the danger. In May 1941, Phillips was therefore made C in C designate of this Far East Fleet, when the opportunity to form it arrived.

Phillips had been dismayed and deeply wounded by the Prime Minister's loss of faith in him. All signs of friendship had departed, and no one had seen them exchange more than formal words since the bitter Greek controversy. Phillips looked forward with relief to the prospect of a sea-going command again, and to leaving behind him rancorous controversies and broken trusts.

There was considerable surprise in the fleet over Tom Phillips's dormant appointment. His reputation as a staff and planning officer could not have been higher. But his name had been linked so closely with that of Pound, and jointly associated with staff work for so long, that the break-up of the partnership was naturally a subject for speculation. The fact that he had not been to sea for some years, and the last time in destroyers, that he had never commanded a battleship, let alone a fleet; that the present C in C China, Admiral Sir Geoffrey Layton, whom he was to relieve, was a most capable and admired commander, all tended to point to other reasons for the appointment. Such is the discretion of the officers of the Royal Navy that very few people discovered them.

When the composition of the Far East Fleet became known late in October, alarm and indignation were aroused, especially in the Home Fleet. Admiral Sir John Tovey, the C in C, wrote to Pound, "I wish to urge as strongly as I can that the dispatch of the *Prince of Wales* to the Far East should not take place. The passage of Atlantic convoys is vital to our existence and their stoppage would rapidly result in our losing the war. There is no comparable interest in the Far East. I am convinced that this proposal involves a risk which cannot be justified under any circumstances even if Japan enters the war." There was some justification for Tovey's alarm. In spite of the Prime Minister's confidence that the *Tirpitz* would not leave the Baltic, the cold fact remained that she might, and that it had taken a naval force of over forty vessels, and eight capital ships and two aircraft carriers, to track down and destroy the *Tirpitz*'s sister ship. If the *Prince of Wales* was taken away from him, Tovey would be left with one battleship at his immediate command, the *King George V*, although other older ones could later be drawn from Force H at Gibraltar in an emergency. In addition, the pocket battleship *Admiral Scheer* was believed to be ready to sail, and there was no certain information on the state of the *Scharnhorst* and *Gneisenau* at Brest. A concerted breakout by these four vessels would have severed the Atlantic trade routes, destroyed millions of tons of shipping, and successfully challenged all that Admiral Tovey could bring to bear against them. It was also pointed out that the *Prince of Wales*, although now commissioned for six months, had still had no opportunity to organise her fighting efficiency. Churchill had exposed his ignorance by claiming that the voyage east would provide a suitable opportunity for her to work-up. Any experienced officer knew that this was an impossibility. Tsar Nicholas II had made the same error of judgment when he had dispatched his four brand new battleships, as the backbone of his Second Pacific Fleet, out to Tsu-Shima in 1904. A warship's company needs time to familiarise themselves with new machinery, instruments and weapons. They need intensive training as a team, and the facilities for target practice, all of which are unavailable on a long voyage. Since they had been thrown into the *Bismarck* pursuit, raw from the dockyard, they had enjoyed none of the leisure required by a ship for efficient working-up.

No time was wasted after the decision of 20 October. Four days later, Tom Phillips took the train to Glasgow, and on the following day he hoisted his flag in the *Prince of Wales*. Greenock and the Clyde estuary were left behind in the afternoon, and the battleship with her escorting destroyers, *Electra* and *Express*, disappeared into the dusk and cold drizzle. On the way out to Cape Town, signals were exchanged between the flagship and the Admiralty about the arrangements to join up with the *Repulse*, which was completing her task of escorting a large convoy via the Cape for the Far East. On 6 November and again on the eighth, Phillips had suggested that he should order the *Repulse* to Ceylon, and there join her before proceeding together to Singapore. The Admiralty approved of these arrangements, which again were not in accord with Pound's proposed compromise that the flagship's movements should be reviewed when she reached Cape Town: an arrangement which had been confirmed with the Prime Minister on 1 November.

Among the Dominion Prime Ministers intimately concerned with the movements of the *Prince of Wales*, was Field-Marshal Smuts, the sagacious visionary who had given such good council to his ex-enemies in one world war, and whose advice was so eagerly sought by Churchill in the second. The Prime Minister evidently thought Phillips might benefit from a talk with Smuts on his way out East, and telegraphed him to introduce Phillips before the arrival of the *Prince of Wales* at Cape Town on 16 November. Churchill referred to Phillips as a great friend and one of our ablest admirals. The South African Prime Minister replied at once that he would be very pleased to see him. A plane was awaiting Phillips at Cape Town, and the admiral was soon flying north to Pretoria. Had Churchill known the nature of Smuts's advice, he would have been less eager to bring about the meeting.

It is clear from the conversations that took place between these two men that, while Smuts was in general agreement that the risk should be taken of depriving the Royal Navy in Home waters of one of its two modern battleships, and of attempting to deter Japan by a show of naval force, he was anxious about the way the operation was to be carried out, and its strategical implications. It was his belief that the maximum publicity and the maximum political advantage should be squeezed from a move that carried with it the gravest risk. If the arrival of the *Prince of Wales* and *Repulse* failed to prevent Japan from attacking southwards and the two ships were present in Singapore or local waters at the outbreak of war, then it was Smuts's opinion that they would certainly be sunk. Their only chance of survival lay in hiding away among the islands of the East Indies, fed by tankers and supply ships that should previously have been placed at scattered fuelling anchorages. Their rôle would then be to instil fear and uncertainty in the enemy by making sporadic raids against Japanese invasion fleets and inferior forces wherever these could be found.

On the day of the *Prince of Wales*'s departure, Smuts expressed his anxiety to Churchill in a telegram which drew attention to the strategic error in dividing American and British Eastern naval strength between Hawaii and Singapore, "two fleets . . . each separately inferior to the Japanese Navy." In going further than this, he became the only statesman, or person of influence, to hint at imminent disaster attaching to Churchill's naval strategy. "If the Japanese are really nippy," he told him, "there is here an opening for a first-class disaster."

There is no record to suggest that Phillips did not agree with Smuts's main thesis, but from what we know of his character, his faith in the power of his big guns as well as his anti-aircraft armament, his self-confidence—and also from the report of his conversations at Pretoria he afterwards gave to his Chief of Staff, Rear-Admiral A. F. E. Palliser—it seems certain that, for the present, he took a slightly more sanguine view than Smuts of their chances of survival.

In order to derive the maximum publicity from his flagship's arrival at the Cape, Phillips had suggested that he should remain in Table Bay for a week, when reporters and photographers would be invited on board and controlled interviews given by officers and crew. These had been carefully planned on the voyage from Britain, and certain officers and men were briefed to describe the *Prince of Wales*'s action against the *Bismarck*, the events on board when she had Churchill as a passenger, and her brief excursion into the Mediterranean, on a Malta convoy, following the Atlantic Conference. But alarm over the political situation continued in London, and the admiral was ordered to leave as soon after forty-eight hours as possible. He therefore flew back from Durban at once, and the *Prince of Wales* left with her two destroyers on 18 November. The reconsideration of her movements promised to Pound never took place, and it was now made known to the whole world that Britain was rapidly building up a Far East Fleet. It was also strongly hinted that her newest battleship was to act as flagship. The news was especially welcomed in Australia and New Zealand.

The *Prince of Wales* made the crossing of the Indian Ocean in ten days, arriving at Colombo on 28 November and dropping anchor within sight of the *Repulse*. The unmodernised battleship *Revenge* was also at Ceylon, as one of the capital ships of the main force the Admiralty still planned to build up in the Indian Ocean over the coming months. Phillips had been asked by the Admiralty what he proposed to do with this vessel, and he told London that he intended to leave her behind when he sailed for Singapore. He gave as his reason for this that the Japanese would interpret a force in Malaya composed of one slow old battleship, a battle cruiser and a fast modern battleship as a perhaps desperate attempt to form some sort of line of battle, whereas the two fast ships alone could only be interpreted as a homogeneous raiding force.

The First Sea Lord had been anxious for "Force Z," as this battle fleet of two capital ships and their escort was now code-named, to leave at once for Singapore so that Phillips could confer with the civil and military authorities there. But two more destroyers, the *Encounter* and *Jupiter*, had not yet arrived from the Mediterranean to complete the escorting half-flotilla, and Churchill protested that the risk of sending away the battle fleet with only the *Express* and *Electra* was not worth the time gained. Phillips therefore took a flying-boat to Singapore, leaving Force Z under the command of Captain William Tennant of the *Repulse*.

The arrival at Singapore on 2 December, 1941, of the *Prince of Wales* and *Repulse* with their escorting destroyers was a historic event in many ways and for many people. It was the last occasion when the influence of the armoured capital ship, as a representation of authority and power, was demonstrated without qualification or compromise. For the Royal Navy, which had for hundreds of years been exerting its pressure in foreign parts against those who threatened Britain's possessions and trade, it was an occasion of agonising significance. For the base and fortress of Singapore, it marked the culmination of more than twenty years' struggle, and the fulfilment at last of the purpose for which certain politicians and military leaders had planned it. Danger of attack from Japan was now imminent, and to deter or resist it the fleet had arrived to lend support to the 15-inch gun batteries. "Main Fleet to Singapore" had been often quoted as a cynical and mocking phrase in the years between the wars, and more frequently than ever since 1939. Now it was there: the Royal Navy's newest battleship, and the handsome, modernised battle cruiser: "HMS *Prince of Wales* and other heavy units . . ." as the official communiqué described them. The fleet was in. "*Kapal perang besar sudar alatang,*" the Malay taxi-drivers were calling out excitedly to one another, across the streets of Singapore, according to *The Times*'s correspondent. The natives streamed down to the shore from the fishing villages flanking the Straits to watch the ships go by, and as the word spread through the city, the people of all races hastened towards the naval base in an attempt to catch a glimpse of the fleet "silhouetted against a background of blue sky and green islands."

The official reception party assembled on a specially built platform alongside newsreel cameramen, radio reporters and correspondents. All those of any civil or military importance in Malaya and the city were present: the tall, elderly figure of Air Marshal Sir Robert Brooke-Popham, overall commander in the Far East, who had been brought back from retirement for this important post; General A. E. Percival, a soft-spoken, slight man, who had been selected as GOC for his patience, intelligence and wide experience as a staff officer; the Governor-General, Sir Shenton Thomas, a distinguished and urbane public servant; Air Vice-Marshal Pulford, commanding the RAF; Alfred Duff-Cooper, Minister of State in the Far East; Admiral Sir Geoffrey Layton, who was shortly to relinquish his command to the small, erect admiral upon whom the safety of Britain's Eastern possessions was now chiefly dependent.

Admiral Phillips looked grey with weariness. The recent anxieties he had undergone and the new responsibilities he carried, added to the continuous strains of the past months, had taxed his nervous reserves to the limit. It was true that in him "the spirit of Drake and Nelson burned with a fierce fire,"[28] and the determination to see through to the end the forlorn task allotted to him had not diminished, but he was now close to breaking under the intolerable burden. He had scarcely had a rest or a clear night's sleep since the beginning of the war. How long he had been taking pills to keep himself going no one knew: perhaps only since the link-up with the *Repulse* and his hasty and hazardous flight from Colombo.

The feelings of the thousands who watched the arrival of the two capital ships on that December afternoon were in striking contrast with Phillips's. A sudden new self-confidence and sense of relief were in the air, and this was felt even by those who knew the real facts about Malaya's land and air defences. There were few who questioned the wisdom of placing so much faith in a pair of capital ships, and perhaps only one or two who recognised the dangers of stationing a lightly supported battle fleet so close to the potential enemy. General Percival was one. His naval staff college course had taught him that this was no balanced fleet. Like Captain Tennant of the *Repulse*, who expressed surprise that no fighter planes had escorted in the battle fleet, he felt concern at the absence of any apparent air support. For not only were there no modern RAF fighters at all in Malaya, but the fleet had failed, after all, to bring an aircraft carrier with them.

Admiral Phillips should have had the brand-new armoured carrier *Indomitable* under his command. But she had accidentally gone aground and damaged herself in the West Indies while working-up. This mishap, which had occurred when the *Prince of Wales* was nine days out of Greenock, was to have a melancholy effect on the course of imminent events: how fundamental can only be speculated. The Admiralty had searched for a replacement, but none could be spared. For political reasons—as well as the stain on the reputation of a new battleship such a reversal would cause—the dispatch of the battle fleet could not now be cancelled for lack of a carrier. Besides, the danger was now so critical that this additional risk had to be accepted. Force Z, it was clear, would have to manage as best it could with whatever air support the RAF could offer.

8 *The Hunt*

Admiral Phillips remained confident that Force Z could successfully defend itself by anti-aircraft fire alone against long-range bomber attack, and against any Japanese threat from the air if fighter protection could be provided. But since he had learned that the aircraft carrier *Indomitable* would not after all be available to him, he had naturally been anxious to discover what the RAF could provide in the way of protection for any operations that he might have to carry out from Singapore. This was the main reason for his hasty departure from Colombo by air, and was the subject of his first conversations after his arrival.

The admiral found Air Vice-Marshal Pulford near to despair about the state of his forces. His constant appeals for more aircraft and for modern machines to replace the old ones under his command had, when they were acknowledged, been met with regretful refusals. For offensive purposes Pulford had thirty-four old light bombers, a handful of American Hudsons, and twenty-seven Vildebeeste torpedo bombers, of such grotesque antiquity—their maximum speed was less than 100 mph—that they made the Swordfish appear a modern machine. When pressed by Phillips for details of the fighter force that might be made available to support raiding fleet operations

of the kind envisaged by Churchill, Pulford reported that
the long-range squadron promised to him and intended to
operate from Singapore had still not materialised, and that
his total operational force for army as well as naval support
consisted of forty-three Brewster Buffaloes. As we have
seen, these had been giving trouble since their arrival from
America, and by European standards were obsolescent. Of
this token force, a full squadron was retained for the defence
of Singapore as a result of pressure from the Governor-
General. The rest operated from the airfields recently
carved out of the Malayan jungle—Alor Star, Kota Bharu,
Gong Kedah, Kuantan and the others—with much difficulty.
Although the C in C Far East, Brooke-Popham, had laid
down that the defence of airfields was to take precedence
over everything except the naval base itself, Pulford had
received few weapons for this purpose, and the anti-aircraft
and ground defences of all the airfields were quite inadequate
to meet determined attack. The real facts of the air situation
in Singapore and the Federated States were far worse even
than Phillips had judged from the figures he had been shown
before his departure. In the event of serious attack, Malaya
possessed no measurable air defence at all.

Phillips discovered that little was known of the strength
and numbers of the enemy. The Naval Intelligence
Department in the Admiralty had been inclined to make a
higher estimate of the quality of Japanese machines and
pilots than Churchill. Information from agents of the
number, performance, carrying power and range of the
bomber forces was very thin. Unconfirmed news of a very
fast and manœuvrable fighter—the Zero—had come through
from China, where they had been seen in action, but

nobody in Singapore was inclined to take this very seriously. The popular view of the troops and the civil population was that Japanese pilots were incompetent, wildly erratic and even suicidal. The old jest that their machines were imitations of western aircraft of First World War vintage, and built largely from bamboo and rice paper, still prevailed, and was taken seriously by many people. Brooke-Popham, in order to counter the anxieties about the peninsula's fighter defences, had stated that Britain "could have her super-Spitfires and hyper-Hurricanes," and that "Buffaloes are good enough for Malaya." This had served further to encourage a low opinion of the Japanese air arm. Phillips's own estimation, according to the official RAF history, was that "the Japanese air forces, both naval and military, were of much the same quality as the Italian and markedly inferior to the Luftwaffe." He also believed, in the light of experience in the Mediterranean and the range and hitting power of British naval torpedo aircraft, that he would be safe from Japanese land-based torpedo aircraft if he operated outside a range of two hundred miles from the new Japanese bases in French Indo-China.

Pulford's information on the aircraft at these airfields was meagre, but he had reason to believe that they were numerous. Phillips already knew about these bases, and how "France's most dastardly deed," as he described it, had completely destroyed the basis on which Malaya's defence system had for years rested, bringing the immediate threat some 1,500 miles nearer to her shores.

Captain Tennant of the *Repulse* was equally anxious to learn about the fighter situation in Malaya. As soon as he could after coming ashore he spoke to Air Vice-Marshal

Pulford, expressing his surprise that none had escorted them into Singapore and that he had not seen one since he had arrived. "If we need it, are you going to be able to provide us with some air cover?" he asked. "Yes, of course," he was told. That evening Tennant dined with his C in C and discussed the fighter position with him. Phillips had the radio tuned in to London, and when the expected announcement of their arrival came over the air he rose from the table and listened with evident pleasure and satisfaction. The tone of the bulletin suggested that, with the arrival of the fleet, the Far East was now secure from possible Japanese aggression. The wording of the official communiqué, which referred to the *Repulse* as "other heavy units," also caused Tennant some concern, not because of its obvious intention to attribute to Force Z a greater strength than it possessed, but for its failure to identify the *Repulse*. Captain Tennant had the highest opinion of the morale and fighting quality of his ship's company, but now they were suffering, after months of sailing without sight of an enemy, the rôle of the anonymous junior partner. The flagship had been the "glamour ship," always in the news, from the *Bismarck* action to the Atlantic Conference, and then on her way out East. Her arrival at Cape Town had been headline news, and in Singapore all the talk was of the *Prince of Wales*. She had led in the fleet, although the *Repulse*'s captain was at the time senior officer, and it was to the flagship that all the attention was given in the ceremonials and celebrations that followed their arrival. HMS "Anonymous," as her own company wryly referred to her, might not have existed. They even had to omit their whereabouts in their censored letters. The next day Tennant mentioned all this to Captain John Leach of the *Prince of Wales*, and he promised to address the *Repulse*'s company to try to explain the reason why, for political reasons, so much publicity had to be given to the flagship.

At the Admiralty in London there was new anxiety at the wide publicity given all over the world to Force Z's arrival in Singapore. The fate of the two capital ships rested on a knife-edge of uncertainty as to how, when, and in what strength, the Japanese would strike. War was clearly imminent. For Sir Dudley Pound these were the most critical and exacting days since hostilities in Europe had begun. Not only had he strongly opposed the dispatch of his newest battleship, but the two conditions of her departure—that she should be accompanied by an aircraft carrier and her destination reviewed en route—had not been met. Now it seemed possible that this weak and unbalanced raiding force of one un-worked-up battleship and one lightly-protected battle cruiser might be trapped in its base or local waters without adequate air cover. Nor was there any evidence that the Prime Minister's earlier announcement that a Far East battle fleet was already being built up had caused any weakening in Tokyo: the result had been quite the reverse of what had been hoped for. On 1 December, even before the arrival of Force Z at Singapore, the Admiralty had telegraphed Phillips suggesting that the two ships should leave the base at once to "disconcert the Japanese, and at the same time increase the security of the force." An intelligence report that Japanese submarines were hovering outside Singapore caused Pound to repeat this suggestion on 3 December. But by then

Phillips had made up his mind that, before taking further steps, he must confer with the American Admiral Hart at Manila in an effort to co-ordinate their actions in the event of sudden attack. On 4 December he flew to the Philippines, in one of the three aircraft capable of making the journey, and there met Admiral Hart, General Douglas MacArthur and the Dutch naval representative.

The conversations between the naval commanders were hamstrung by political restrictions. While Britain had agreed to support the United States if she were attacked, no reciprocal arrangement had been reached. It was not certain, therefore, that the United States Asiatic Fleet of cruisers, destroyers and submarines, and the Dutch naval squadron, would even be involved if Japan struck only at Malaya. Hart was chiefly concerned with keeping open his supply lines from Hawaii and the United States itself, and MacArthur did his best to persuade Phillips to bring his battle fleet to the Philippines. If the Japanese landed in the Philippines, he told the British C in C, he would throw them out, and if they delayed their invasion by six months they would not even be able to land. In spite of the difficulties under which the talks were held, general agreement was reached in the short time available on the matter of ship dispositions and the co-ordination of operations. The British capital ships were to operate as a striking force against any Japanese movement towards Malaya, the Malay barrier and the Dutch East Indies. The mixed American, British, Australian and Dutch cruiser force would be used to keep open communications in the Australia, Singapore, Philippines and Dutch East Indies area. There would be no overall commander.

This makeshift arrangement for the hopelessly inadequate naval forces available for the defence of this rich area, on which Japan would depend for her supplies of oil, rubber and numerous vital minerals in time of war, was all that time and political circumstances allowed.

While Admiral Phillips was talking with Admiral Hart in Manila—and the Japanese transports were completing their loading before setting off across the Gulf of Siam—Captain Tennant was engaged on a flag-showing operation to Australia. This Dominion had been in an acutely sensitive condition for some months, caused by the apparent neglect of its defence by Britain while her own servicemen were in great numbers in Britain and were fighting for the Empire in the Middle East. The arrival of the battle fleet in Singapore had reassured Canberra, and to emphasise further Britain's concern for the safety of Australia, the *Repulse* had been ordered to Port Darwin for a short stay. As she left, a pair of Brewster Buffaloes wheeled briefly overhead. They were the first Captain Tennant had seen.

The Intelligence authorities in Singapore received the first definite news of the departure of a Japanese invasion fleet on the morning of 6 December. For political reasons, Brooke-Popham decided that no military action should be taken against it, and even the precautionary long-planned defensive "Operation Matador" should not be put into effect in case the Japanese destination was only Siam. But from Phillips's naval headquarters in Singapore his Chief of Staff, Admiral Palliser, telegraphed the information urgently to Manila, and ordered the return of the *Repulse*. Air-

Marshal Pulford sent off on reconnaissance a squadron of Australian Hudsons from the airfield of Kota Bharu in the far north of Malaya. At 2 pm at the very limit of their operating range, the Hudsons radioed back confirmation and details of the Japanese Fleet. They had identified two great convoys steaming west. One was of twenty-two merchant ships, averaging 10,000 tons, escorted by a battleship, five cruisers and seven destroyers; the other was made up of twenty-one merchantmen with twelve more warships as escort. Both had reached a point some eighty miles east-south-east of the southern tip of Indo-China. The Hudsons were later relieved by a pair of Catalina flyingboats, one of which was shot down. This first act of hostility, some nine hours before Pearl Harbor, marked the opening of the Pacific War.

All through the summer of 1941 Rear-Admiral Sadaichi Matsunaga's 22nd Air Flotilla had been carrying out an intensive sea-attack training programme from their airfields in South Formosa. Many of the pilots had already seen action in China and had carried out attacks against Chinese shipping. Their future targets were likely to be more heavily and skilfully defended, however, and this prolonged course was intended to prepare the crews for the time when they would have to meet the fire of British and American warships and fighters. The 22nd Naval Air Flotilla was formed from three corps, the Mihoro and Genzan each equipped with forty-eight "Nell" bombers, and the Kanoya corps with forty-eight "Bettys." All these twin-engined machines were equipped to carry either 250, 500, or 800 kg. bombs, or the Type 91 torpedo, with an explosive war-head of either 150 or 205 kgs. The flotilla also included thirty-six "Zeke" fighters, and a reconnaissance flight of six "Babs" machines.

In October the Mihoro and Genzan corps flew south to Indo-China by way of Hainan Island, landing at the ex-French airfields of Thudaumot and Soctrang, north and south of Saigon, which housed the flotilla's headquarters. Training was continued until late in November, when news filtered through from Intelligence that two British capital ships had left Colombo heading for Singapore. One of them was believed to be Britain's most modern battleship. Besides seven heavy and two light cruisers with supporting destroyers, the Navy Department had made provision for only two Japanese capital ships for the Malay invasion. The old *Kongo* and *Haruna* would have been perfectly adequate to deal with British heavy cruisers known to be available for Singapore from Australia and the East Indies; they could certainly not be expected to survive alone against a new British battleship supported by a battle cruiser. The Navy Department therefore determined to increase still further its naval air power in this area, and before the *Prince of Wales* and *Repulse* had arrived, three more front-line squadrons had been ordered down from Formosa. These were twenty-seven "Bettys" of the Kanoya corps. To support the landing operations and to attack any British naval force attempting to interfere with them, Admiral Matsunaga therefore had at his disposal one hundred and twenty-three of the most advanced naval attack aircraft, and highly trained crews, in the world.

During the first days of December single aircraft of the flotilla were sent out on patrol across the Gulf of Siam as far south as Singapore. They saw no shipping and caught only an occasional glimpse of a British reconnaissance machine. The planes sheered away in mutual embarrassment on these occasions. On 3 December the two British capital ships were seen far below in the naval base at Singapore. One had six heavy guns in three turrets, the other ten guns, eight of them quadrupled, and a pair. They could only be the *Renown* or *Repulse* and one of the new *King George V* class battleships. Confirmation of the identity of the larger vessel was provided by British Press and radio reports.

On 2 December squadron commanders were informed that the long-awaited war on Britain and America would begin from midnight on 7-8 December. The keenest excitement mounted among the air crews as the hour approached for which they had trained since the beginning of their service careers. They were all confident in their machines, their weapons, and their own skill. Soon after 11 pm on the night of 7 December, the Mihoro and Genzan corps took off to bomb Singapore while the first transports went ashore on the north Malay coast. It was a stormy, cloud-infested night, and the "Nells," flying in close formation of six squadrons of nine, were forced to switch on navigation lights to keep station. Intermittently the lightning flashed out from the cumulo-nimbus and the crews saw it reflected from the propeller blades of their machines. The weather became worse as they flew farther south across the South China Sea, until the "Nells" were forced to break their formation. At about 2 am Matsunaga regretfully ordered their recall. The Mihoro corps disregarded the order, however, and carried on through the thick cloud. They were rewarded by clear skies over the city. Ten thousand feet below the lights were blazing and they had no difficulty in locating their targets. No fighters were seen, and the anti-aircraft fire was light and inaccurate. The bombers returned through a clear, calm dawn, and when they landed they heard the first news of the successful landing on the Malay coast. One of the squadron commanders, Lieutenant Sadao Takai, was approached by a French officer, still stationed on the airfield, and congratulated on the Japanese attack on Pearl Harbor, the news of which had just come through.

Later on 8 December, Admiral Matsunaga called together all squadron leaders to consider the best means of attacking the two British capital ships. A "Babs" reconnaissance machine had been over Singapore and reported that they were still in harbour and undamaged by the night's bombing. There was curiosity at this failure of the Royal Navy to interfere with the landing operations at Kota Bharu, and it was decided that an attack must be made on them to prevent their departure. At all costs, the pilots were told, the battle fleet had to be destroyed, and the damage that could be caused to Japanese transports and warships if they failed was again emphasised. Details of the depth of water in the naval base were asked for at this conference, and the most advantageous height and direction of attack were discussed. But the bombers never took off. That evening Japanese Intelligence learnt that the *Prince of Wales* and the battle cruiser had left.

Admiral Palliser's signal to Captain Tennant had read, "Return with all dispatch." No reason had been given for the sudden recall of the *Repulse*, and her captain needed none. It was obvious that war was only hours away. A sharp lookout was kept for Japanese planes, but the ocean appeared as deserted from the battle cruiser as it had to the 22nd Air Corps pilots on their reconnaissance patrols. The *Repulse* was no longer capable of the thirty-one knots she had reached on her trials twenty-four years earlier. The weight of her additional armour plate and high-angle guns, with their ammunition, the radar and numerous other additions, had all increased her draft, and her turbines now vibrated roughly at high revolutions. She was due for a refit and rebuild in an American yard, and when he had learnt that this would have to be postponed, Captain Tennant had asked his Chief Engineer if he thought her engines would last out. "They'll just about make it," he was told. Like most old and devotedly nursed marine machinery, they rose to the occasion magnificently, and the *Repulse* cut north through calm seas at twenty-seven knots after the recall.

The flying-boat from Manila arrived back with Admiral Phillips twenty-four hours after the *Repulse* secured behind the *Prince of Wales* again on the afternoon of December 6. An Admiralty signal was awaiting him. It read: "On assumption that Japanese expedition in South China Sea on course indicating invasion, report what action would be possible to take with naval or air forces." The assumption was realised within hours. Soon after midnight on 7-8 December, the first confirmed reports of Japanese landings in Siam and on the northern Malay coast were arriving at Singapore, and the 22nd Air Flotilla's bombers were over the city soon after 4 am, providing the *Prince of Wales*'s

high-angle gun crews with some much-needed practice.
It was now clear beyond any doubt, to Phillips as well as
to Pound and the Board of Admiralty in London, that not
only had the coming of the fleet to Singapore failed to deter,
but that the two capital ships had been caught in an
agonising tactical trap from which there might be no
escape.

An answer to the question posed by the Admiralty signal
of 7 December was sought at a conference held the next day
at 12.30 in Admiral Phillips's "cuddy" in the *Prince of Wales*.
There were present at this crucial meeting, besides Phillips
himself in the chair, his Chief of Staff, Captain Leach
commanding the flagship, Captain Tennant, the Captain
of the Fleet, and a number of senior staff officers. The
temperature and humidity were high, even for Singapore
at noon in mid-summer, and the officers in their tropical
uniform and white drill shorts had not yet accustomed
themselves to the equatorial conditions, especially below
armoured steel decks in an inadequately ventilated battleship.

The portent and drama of the gathering were inescapable.
Admiral Phillips himself looked ill, and his grey face was
damp with sweat. Concisely and in sharp tones he outlined
the military situation. The Japanese landings at Kota Bharu,
Singora, Tepha and Patani had all succeeded. The army
was being hard-pressed and was falling back. RAF losses
had already been heavy. Two Japanese capital ships, and
a strong force of heavy cruisers were known to be in the
Gulf of Siam on protective duties. It had to be presumed
that reinforcements would be landed and that the routes

between Indo-China and the Siam-Malaya coastline would be thick with transports.

After sending the junior staff officers out of the cabin, Phillips outlined his plan for a raiding trip up the east coast of Malaya. When he had completed his outline, he looked round at those who remained and asked them, "Now what do you think of this plan?" There was a period of silence, which Tennant thought to have lasted half a minute, before he recognised it as his duty, as captain of the only other capital ship in the fleet, to express his views.

"We've come to secure our communications," he said. "That was our purpose. Now that we're here, I don't see what possible alternative we have but to do as you have proposed."

There were, in fact, two alternative courses open to them. One was to remain where they were; the other was to retreat. To remain tied up passively in their base after their triumphant arrival and while the army and RAF were fighting so desperately in the north, was not to be contemplated. It might be possible in later years to argue, in cold strategic terms, that the disappearance of the battle fleet into the Indian Ocean where it could exert a threatening influence on Japanese operations would have been a wise move. But a defensive rôle of this nature was objectionable to the deeply-rooted service philosophy of all the officers present, and especially to Phillips himself. It was alien to their closed world of unquestioned loyalties and rigid values. Such a course could have been chosen only after the most unemotional calculation. And emotion—bellicose and vengeful—was strongly present at that meeting.

There were murmurs of concurrence from the other

officers. Phillips nodded and at once began to describe his intentions in greater detail. The fleet would leave with four destroyers shortly before dusk, for security reasons and in the hope of evading enemy submarine patrols off Singapore. It would proceed east of the Anambas Islands to avoid minefields, then turn north to a point about 150 miles south of Cape Cambodia and well beyond a range of 200 miles from the nearest Japanese airfields at Saigon. The intention was to arrive at dawn on 10 December off Singora, destroy the enemy transports and escorting warships, and then proceed at best speed down the coast back to base. The success of the expedition, he explained, depended on surprise, speed, fighter protection over the scene of the intended raid, and air reconnaissance northward of his course. With these provisions met, he thought there was a good chance of destroying further land reinforcements and cutting off supplies to those already ashore. With their 14-inch and 15-inch guns they could cause immense destruction.

The meeting broke up before lunch, and Phillips at once signalled his intentions to London. Then he dispatched in writing a request to Air Vice-Marshal Pulford for:

"A. Reconnaissance 100 miles to north of Force daylight 9th December.

"B. Reconnaissance 100 miles mid point Singora 10 miles from coast starting first light 10th December.

"C. Fighter protection off Singora at daylight 10th December."

as air support for the raiding expedition.

From the uncertain and spasmodic information that was percolating back to Singapore, Pulford knew that all his

more northerly airfields were suffering from vigorous
attack which they were almost helpless to resist. Kota
Bharu in particular had been heavily and almost continuously bombed since dawn by aircraft already established
at Singora, and there was only a handful of undamaged
aircraft remaining. Pulford had no means of calculating
how many Buffalo fighters he would have left forty hours
hence, nor whether he would still have in his hands the
airfields from which to operate them. Their useful range
was less than two hundred miles, and he did not feel able to
promise fighter cover as far north as Singora at dawn on
10 December, although he would do his best to comply.
At about four o'clock that afternoon Pulford therefore
informed Phillips that he should be able to provide Force Z
with the reconnaissance he needed but could not be certain
about the fighter protection. Within half an hour Pulford
had received a telegram from the officer commanding
Kota Bharu requesting permission to withdraw his
ground forces and remaining aircraft as the airfield was
no longer tenable. At 5.35 the *Prince of Wales* and *Repulse*
sailed.

Among the senior officers who had attended the last
conference in the *Prince of Wales* and who understood the
realities of the situation, there developed during that hot,
busy afternoon a sense of unreality and fatalism. The
first news of a devastating attack on the American Pacific
Fleet at Pearl Harbor, an hour and a half after the Malayan
invasion, had now been received in Singapore. The details
were uncertain and contradictory, but already it was clear
that both British and American Intelligence had seriously

underestimated the skill and striking power of the Japanese naval air arm. The hazards they would be facing during this four-days-long raiding expedition were many and sinister in their uncertainty. Their frail destroyer screen, the defence provided by their own guns and armour and perhaps by a few obsolete RAF fighters, were all they possessed to resist the threat of submarines, which were known to be out in strength, land-based and perhaps carrier-based aircraft, mines and the gunfire of a formidable Japanese surface fleet.

Admiral Layton, who had formally handed over to Phillips as C in C Far East only that morning, and was due to leave in forty-eight hours on the liner *Dominion Monarch*, has described the evening departure of the two capital ships as a pathetic sight. He had many old friends on board and did not expect to see any of them again, least of all his successor as C in C, the small, anguished figure of Tom Phillips. Captain Tennant, who had known John Leach of the *Prince of Wales* for many years and greatly admired his qualities as a staff officer, found time during the afternoon to bid him a sombre farewell. Their mutual anxiety remained unspoken, and each returned to his ship to draft out a message and briefing to his men. The nature and tone of Tennant's rightly presumed that none of the apprehension felt by the senior officers had reached the lower decks, where even the oppressive heat had failed to subdue their eagerness for action.

"For two months past," Captain Tennant told his men, "the ship has felt that she has been deprived of her fair share of hitting the enemy. Although we have been constantly at sea and steamed 53,000 miles in nine months,

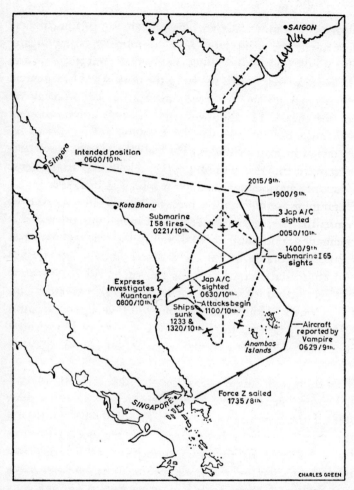

General map showing the course of Force Z from
December 8th to December 10th 1941

we have seen practically nothing. There is every possibility that things are going to change completely. . . . We are off to look for trouble. I expect we shall find it. . . . We are going to carry out a sweep to the northward to see what we can pick up and what we can roar up. We must all be on our toes." He followed this cheering announcement with an appeal to his men not to allow themselves to be distracted from their duties. He had already seen how easy it was for men whose duties lay elsewhere to become spectators and neglect their own job. "When, say, high-range guns are engaging a high-flying aircraft and all eyes are in the sky, none of the short-range guns on the disengaged side should be looking at the engagement but should be standing-by for a low dive-bombing or torpedo-bombing attack coming from the other side." Tennant had every confidence in the men who had served under him for so long. "I know the old ship will give a good account of herself," he told them. "May each one of us, without exception, keep calm if and when action comes. . . ."

The deep red sun was low in the sky and sharply silhouetting the shoreline palm trees when the two ships slipped their moorings, proceeded down the Straits of Johore, through the boom, and into the open sea. The battle fleet's departure was as unobtrusive as its arrival had been spectacular. Few people in Singapore knew that the two ships with their escort had even gone to sea, and only two reporters and a photographer had been invited on the raid. The reports were O. D. Gallagher of the *Daily Express* and the American Cecil Brown. At first the *Repulse* led the way, and then she yielded her place to the *Prince of*

Wales, which overtook her. For a few moments the two great ships, dour and purposeful in their daubed camouflage paint, stripped for action and with their high-angle guns already pointing skywards, sailed abeam of each other. The upper decks were lined with men. Phillips and his Flag Captain were on the bridge of the flagship. As they slipped ahead Tennant saluted and waved to them, and the C in C and Leach waved back with their caps.

A signal from the flagship as a precaution against mines ordered "stand by paravanes." Course was north-east, speed seventeen knots, the two big ships still in line ahead four cables apart, with the destroyers ahead and on each flank. Darkness fell suddenly, and almost at once the stars were obscured by a cloud sheet. The barometer was falling rapidly and dirty weather was forecast for the next day. It soon became known that Force Z would need all the concealment provided by poor weather conditions, for at 10.53 the *Prince of Wales* received from Admiral Palliser, who had remained ashore to look after Phillips's office in Singapore, a fateful and momentous signal. "Fighter protection on Wednesday 10th," it ran, "will not, repeat not, be possible." Nor could more reconnaissance than that provided by a single Catalina be promised. Palliser had heard from Pulford that Kota Bharu airfield had now been evacuated. He had also learnt from Intelligence that the Japanese bomber force in southern Indo-China was even more formidable than had at first been estimated. This news, too, he passed on to Phillips. Before Force Z was a hundred miles from its base, therefore, it was thus deprived of two of the conditions on which, in Phillips's estimation, the success of the operation depended. At once the element of risk had been immeasurably increased and the opportunity for surprise greatly reduced.

Nevertheless Admiral Phillips decided to continue with the operation. Success now must depend on their remaining unobserved throughout daylight hours of 9 December, or to the time when they would alter course west towards Singora. They would, if necessary, then leave behind their destroyers, whose operating range at high speed was restricted, and make for the coast at full speed through the hours of darkness, hoping to mix in with the Japanese invasion forces at dawn.

The result of Phillips's deliberations during the night of 8-9 December was evident in the signal to all ships' companies of Force Z issued by the C in C in the morning. It contained no hint of new anxieties.

"The enemy has made several landings on the north coast of Malaya and has made local progress," he began. "Our army is not large and is hard pressed in places. Our air force has had to destroy and abandon one or more aerodromes. Meanwhile fast transports lie off the coast.

"This is our opportunity before the enemy can establish himself. We have made a wide circuit to avoid air reconnaissance and hope to surprise the enemy shortly after sunrise to-morrow, Wednesday. We may have the luck to try our metal against the old Japanese battle cruiser *Kongo* or against some Japanese cruisers and destroyers which are reported in the Gulf of Siam. We are sure to get some useful practice with the HA armament.

"Whatever we meet I want to finish quickly and so get well clear to the eastward before the Japanese can mass too formidable a scale of an attack against us. So shoot to sink."

Tactical instructions to ships' commanders, specifying speeds, range of fire in battle and granting the *Repulse* freedom of manœuvre at the C in C's discretion, followed this information to ships' companies, and the need for vigilance and avoidance of enemy reconnaissance was again emphasised.

The continued secrecy of their progress towards the target area, and the immense destructive power of their big guns: these were the remaining factors that could still tell in their favour. If the low clouds, driving rain and poor visibility that prevailed at dawn on 9 December continued throughout the day, then there appeared still to be a chance of achieving surprise and success. Among cruiser- or destroyer-escorted transports the capital ships' 15-inch and 14-inch guns could then wreak immense havoc in a matter of minutes. There would then remain only the full speed race back to base. "Having stirred up a hornet's nest, we must expect plenty of bombing," as Tennant warned his men. They might even be overwhelmed. But if both were sent to the bottom, and the men perished without a survivor, the raid would have justified itself if it resulted in the crushing of the Malayan invasion.

There was a passing moment of crisis soon after dawn, at 6.20 am when a lookout in the destroyer *Vampire* reported having sighted briefly through the low mist and swirling clouds an unidentified aircraft. Before any confirmation could be obtained, the machine had vanished, and Phillips decided to disregard the report. For the rest of the morning and afternoon the weather continued to favour them. Hot rain squalls scudded over the ships, followed by a fine driving mist. There were sudden lifts in the cloud level, momentarily revealing higher cumulus, then it would close warmly and comfortingly about them again. But never for a moment during those long daylight hours could they feel secure beneath this ever-moving tropical curtain that seemed as if it might at any time be drawn treacherously aside to reveal the white scar-line of a periscope or the small cross of a distant searching aircraft above them. At 12.45 there was another sudden alarm that brought the heavy high-angle and pom-pom barrels swinging effortlessly around on their greased mountings. This time the aircraft was close, large and clumsy-looking, muzzily silhouetted through the mist. It was a Catalina, one of the remaining pair possessed for long-range search by the RAF, perhaps the very one providing their reconnaissance. It came in brave and low over the flagship, flashing by Aldis lamp at the bridge: "Japanese making landing north of Singora." It was the best news they could hope for. That was their destination, in another eighteen hours, just as the transports would be turning round.

Many of the men had already performed the old pre-battle ritual of changing into clean clothes against wound infection. The anti-aircraft gun crews and others who expected soon to be exposed to shell or bomb flash, had slipped on over their shorts and shirts old long-sleeved sweaters and long socks, overalls, or heavy duffel-coats. Beside them and ready for immediate use were their tin helmets and the thick, heavy anti-flash hoods and gloves. By noon the men of the two big ships and the four escorting destroyers all appeared equipped for Arctic duty.

At 4.30 that afternoon Force Z was some 170 miles from the southernmost point of Indo-China and on the same latitude as the Siam-Malaya border and Kota Bharu. In two hours' time, when the light began to fail, the ships would swing eighty degrees to port for the night-long rush to the coast. The sky remained overcast, each threatening cloud break closing in again to seal them off from the clear skies above. Bursts of rain continued to spray across the decks and over the exposed high-angle gun crews in sudden cooling sweeps.

It was not until after five o'clock that the weather finally proved its treachery, dissolving its opacity to reveal the force in all its helpless vulnerability. As on any English storm-racked summer day, the low clouds seemed suddenly to peel away with the approach of dusk. The mist lifted, and the low-lying sun on the port horizon shimmered suddenly and dazzlingly across the wave tops, turning the sullen Turner seascape into a sharp etching.

The planes were there, as the men of Force Z knew they would be, poised threateningly in the north as if hung from the sky. First one, then two, and then three were reported, only just discernible and far out of range, observing them at indecent leisure, confident in their invulnerability.

9 Carnage at Noon

THE FINE CALCULATIONS that guided the decisions of Admiral Sir Tom Phillips from the time his battle fleet sailed from Singapore on the evening of 8 December were governed by the need to injure the enemy and procure the survival of his two heavy units. From the first, the risk element was almost unacceptably high. From the time when the C in C knew he could have no fighter protection, he had judged that they would continue only if they were unobserved during the hours of daylight. By 5.30 that evening he knew that all chances of surprise had been lost. The enemy, forewarned of their approach, would scatter their transport convoys and concentrate their surface and submarine forces for counter-attack. If he persisted with his plan there was a strong chance of enemy bombing attack. He did not doubt that his big ships would survive these, as capital ships at sea had always survived even the most intense air attacks since the beginning of the war. It was the risk of receiving an injury which might slow them up that he had to consider; the kind of offensive action on which British naval air strategy was based, and which had proved so successful against the *Bismarck* and the Italian fleet at Matapan. The success of the raid, he believed, rested from the beginning on Force Z's speed of retirement.

Even a small injury to one of his capital ships could restrict their powers of manœuvre in a surface action, and increase their vulnerability to submarine and destroyer attack, perhaps resulting in the loss of them both.

These were considerations that must have preoccupied the mind of the admiral as Force Z continued north at seventeen knots towards Indo-China. Even now, in spite of his earlier determination to turn back if his battle fleet were sighted, he found a decision hard to reach. To retreat in face of the enemy, to return empty-handed from a raid of which so much had been expected, to abstain from joining the battle in which the two other services were being so sorely tried, were all bitter prospects to face, and were antagonistic to the highest naval principles. Phillips's action, in ordering the return of his force to Singapore, was perhaps the most courageous in a brilliant and distinguished career. At 6.35 pm he sent the old destroyer *Tenedos*, already due to leave them because of her restricted range, back to base and to signal Admiral Palliser with a request for all available destroyers at Singapore to be sent out to meet them. In order to deceive the enemy about their true position, this radio message was not to be transmitted until eight o'clock the following morning when the *Tenedos* would be well clear of the main force. To confuse still further the enemy, whose reconnaissance machines still lingered close to the skyline far to the north, Phillips also ordered their original plan to be adhered to until after dark. Accordingly, Force Z continued north until 7 pm, when course was altered to north-west and speed increased to twenty-six knots as if the dash to the coast had begun.

It was not until 8 pm that the *Repulse* was informed of

the cancellation of the operation, and darkness had fallen before the turn south was made and speed reduced to conserve the fuel of the remaining destroyers. The news was received with bitter disappointment by the battle cruiser's men, most of whom were young volunteers, who had steamed so far and for so long on so many abortive operations before, and had been led to believe that this time, at last, they were going to see some action. In the *Repulse*'s wardroom feelings were mixed. The disappointment was as keen, but the officers' closer appreciation of their real situation, provided by their knowledge of the facts and their long professional training, led them to accept the correctness of their C in C's decision. "It isn't worth risking two capital ships under the strategic circumstances," was the comment of Commander Dendy, and Captain Tennant signalled his admiral that he agreed entirely with his decision.

Like Admiral Rozhestvensky's Second Pacific Fleet thirty-six years earlier, the last hours of Admiral Phillips's Force Z were marked with a series of tragic ironies that, together, decided its fate. A few more minutes steaming on their northerly course would have brought the battle fleet within sight and range of a force of four Japanese heavy cruisers that were then only fifteen miles distant and surely must have succumbed to the big guns of the British capital ships in an engagement. The reconnaissance aircraft first spotted by the lookouts of the *Prince of Wales* were not from the 22nd Air Flotilla but were seaplanes launched from the catapults of the cruisers *Kinu* and *Kumano* of this force, under the command of Admiral Kuritas. If they saw the British force, no word of their sighting was received by the 22nd Air Flotilla.

At Admiral Matsunaga's headquarters in Saigon, and at his bases, there was already intense activity. Here preparations were being made for a massive attack of quite a different kind on Force Z, which they believed to be three hundred miles farther south. Only that morning a reconnaissance plane had returned from Singapore claiming to have found and identified the *Prince of Wales* and *Repulse* still at their base after all. The entire corps was therefore at once briefed for a concentrated raid on the ships before they could leave. The "Bettys" and "Nells" were about to take off when a signal was received from naval headquarters which caused a complete reversal of plans. At two o'clock that afternoon, unknown to Phillips, whose destroyers' asdic had failed to locate it, the Japanese submarine I65 had glimpsed the shapes of the big ships steaming north through the mist. When they were gone from sight the submarine had surfaced and radioed the information, which had reached Saigon at 3.40 pm. The news came as a complete surprise to Matsunaga, but further credence was given to the submarine's report when the aerial photographs of Singapore harbour taken by the reconnaissance plane were found to show that the observer had mistaken two large merchantmen for the capital ships. Spurred on by the knowledge of the extreme and now imminent danger to their transports and naval forces, the ground crews of the three corps therefore hastened to unload the bombs from their aircraft and replace them with Mk I and Mk II Type 91 torpedoes. This laborious and difficult operation was completed by 6.30 pm, as night was falling.

All the flotilla's aircraft were airborne by seven o'clock, just as Force Z altered course towards the west and increased speed.

The difficulties in finding and attacking with torpedoes on a moonless night a powerful enemy fleet were recognised and accepted at Japanese headquarters, and by the aircrews. The risks were high, but the danger to the transports off Singora was now so critical that almost any casualty rate was acceptable to prevent an attack that could compromise the entire Malayan operation. The weather closed in again even before the aircraft reached the coast, and orders were given for the air fleet to spread out over the area between the point where the battle fleet had last been seen, and its likely target areas off Kota Bharu and Singora. The "Nells" and "Bettys" formed up in flights of three instead of their usual squadron formation of nine, flying with navigation lights on above cloud, in the hope of finding a break, or at less than a thousand feet below it and through intermittent rain squalls, where their range of visibility was necessarily restricted to a small radius. The chances of discovering a blacked out enemy force in this vast area appeared hopeless to the pilots. Apart from the dangers of collision, it was also possible that they would confuse their own naval forces, also keenly searching the same area, with those of the enemy. At one point a Mihoro crew radioed that they had located a large warship and were dropping a flare over it before attacking. Seconds later, and even before nearby aircraft could alter course towards the position, they added that the flare had revealed the cruiser *Chokai*, flagship of Vice-Admiral Ozawa. A short time after this, Matsunaga regretfully ordered the recall of all his aircraft so that they could be refuelled for a continuation of the search at dawn. He was as aware as Admiral Phillips that the successful interception of the battle fleet on the following day might again depend on the weather.

But the air service had under-estimated the reconnaissance skill of the fleet's submarine commanders. In little less than an hour after the last of the twin-engined "Bettys" and "Nells" had touched down to their difficult full-load landing in the dark, a signal that was again to alter the whole search situation arrived from naval headquarters. In total darkness at 2.20 on the morning of 10 December, another submarine, the I58, suddenly found herself almost in the path of the oncoming battle fleet. This time there could be no doubt of the ships' identity, for they were far south of the searching Japanese Navy vessels. I58's commander crash-dived and just had time to fire a salvo of five torpedoes, all of which missed, at one of the big ships as it sped past. Then the submarine surfaced, radioed her exciting news, and took up the pursuit at her maximum surface speed. But at that time Force Z, which had also recently received a message of great importance—and one which was again to bring about another dramatic turn to events—was proceeding at twenty-four knots. This was eight knots faster than the submarine could manage, and at 3.05 am, I58 lost sight of the battle fleet in the darkness.

The signal from this submarine caused considerable confusion at Japanese naval headquarters. They had correctly estimated Force Z's destination as being Singora, or perhaps Kota Bharu. Now it was known that the British Fleet was hastening back, apparently on a reverse course. There were no targets for the enemy's guns south of latitude 5 degrees north; it seemed certain, therefore, that the raiding foray had been abandoned. Already the British force was too far south for interception by Japanese surface vessels, and these were therefore sent back to their base at Kamranh Bay.

The responsibility for the destruction of the two capital ships now rested entirely with the aircraft of the 22nd Air Flotilla and their air crews. If battle was to ensue, it would be the biggest-ever contest between air and sea power in the armoured battleship's life; the most crucial torpedo versus capital ship engagement of all time.

By the time the hunters had made the assumption that the raiding designs of Force Z had been abandoned, it was no longer valid. For at midnight a message had been received from Singapore which suggested to Admiral Phillips that, in spite of the cancellation of the original raid, even richer targets for the big guns might after all be awaiting them farther south. In Phillips's office at the naval base, Admiral Palliser had no knowledge that the C in C had called off the raid when he dispatched a further warning signal to Force Z soon after nine o'clock that "enemy bombers on South Indo-China aerodromes are in force and undisturbed. They could attack you five hours after sighting and much depends on whether you have been seen to-day." Palliser added that there might also be two aircraft carriers in the area. This was Phillips's first news that his force was perhaps also within range of carrier planes, but there was little else of interest in this message. Palliser's next signal, however, was momentous. "Enemy reported landing Kuantan, latitude 03 degrees

50 north," it ran. No indication of the authority for this report was given.

Another major landing half-way down the Malayan coastline was at once recognised by Phillips as a sound strategical move for the Japanese to make, and a desperately dangerous one for the defending British forces. From Kuantan there ran the only major road bisecting the Federated States. Possession of this road by the enemy would cut off all General Percival's troops fighting in the north, and bring the threat to Singapore itself more than 150 miles nearer. A rapid navigational reckoning showed the C in C that, by increasing speed and altering course to the south-west, the *Prince of Wales* and *Repulse* could be off Kuantan soon after dawn, perhaps at the most vulnerable moment of disembarkation. Good fortune had, it seemed, after all decided to favour this expedition. Moreover, at Kuantan they could reasonably expect fighter cover, for they were just within range of the Singapore squadron of Buffaloes.

Still confident that he had, by his speed and direction at nightfall, deceived the enemy as to his whereabouts and intentions, Phillips continued to maintain radio silence. He believed that surprise could still be achieved on this new raid; and he had no doubt that, had he been in Admiral Palliser's place, he would have presumed that Force Z would now make directly for Kuantan, an obviously rich and top priority target area. Admiral Palliser was a good staff officer of long experience. In Phillips's estimation, he would, therefore, understand his C in C's reaction and automatically make provision for fighter cover off the coast of Kuantan at dawn without the need for a specific request that would reveal the fleet's position. These were the thoughts that Admiral Phillips expressed to his staff during the early hours of that anxious morning. The conclusions were those of a highly intelligent officer who had himself spent a great part of his career on staff work and expected an equal degree of insight and intelligence from his subordinates.

After course was altered towards Kuantan at 12.50 am, Force Z maintained its high speed for the remainder of the night, again failing to observe the Japanese submarine, as well as the torpedoes that were this time aimed at them from it. Dawn began to break at 5 am, revealing a clear sky of dull grey and mauve hues that faded only when a huge red sun arose slowly out of the sea behind them. For a while it seemed to give no heat, and the air was strangely thin. The horizon was sharp and distant on every side. Hovering above it, as if it had hung there tied to them by an invisible strand through the night, was a single enemy reconnaissance plane.

There was little time for any sleep for the air crews of the 22nd Air Flotilla, and none at all for the ground staff on the night of 9-10 December. The last plane landed at about 2.30 am; soon after 6.00 am the first machines of the new attack were taking off in the cool dawn air, climbing steadily with their heavy load as they disappeared to the south. There were twelve of them in all, three "Babs" reconnaissance machines and a full squadron from the Genzan corps carrying 600 kg. bombs. All were to carry out a sector search based on the estimated position, speed and course of the British fleet. The tactical plan drawn up by Matsunaga was to open the attack with high level bombing to demoralise the British crews and damage the upper works of the the ships, and then alternate bombing with torpedo attacks in rapid succession, the first to distract and cause casualties among the high-angle gunners as well as to start fires, the second to commit the serious damage to the hulls of the ships.

Between 7.35 and 9.30 am, thirty-four bomb-carrying "Nells" and twenty-six "Nells" and the same number of "Bettys" loaded with torpedoes, all took off from their Saigon bases, forming up in squadrons of nine. Five aircraft in addition to the reserves, failed through various causes to make up the correct numbers and join in the attack; but there remained for the striking force ninety-five aircraft in all. There was no apparent evidence of weariness among the air crews, although after some seventy-two hours of the most strenuous operations this would have been forgivable. The lunch they took with them for this flight, which was certain to be long and arduous, was of *ohagi*, or bean paste-coated rice cake, and coffee syrup in Thermos flasks.

Except for the first Genzan squadron, which had been briefed to bomb from 8000 feet, all the aircraft flew off on their pre-determined course at between 10,000 and 12,000 feet, their most economical operating altitude, and with the leanest setting of their mixture controls in order to economise fuel. All the pilots had long experience of nursing their fuel supplies, an essential requirement for the long-range Pacific operations for which their machines were intended. This was particularly important for the torpedo planes which carried thirty per cent less fuel than the bombers to compensate for the extra weight of their weapons.

For the first time since the Malayan invasion, the weather was clear, and as the formations left Cape Cambodia behind them and spread out over the South China Sea they saw that conditions were at last in their favour. They were, in fact, perfect for this type of operation, with sufficient scattered cloud at 1000 to 1700 feet to provide cover without obstructing seriously their range of visibility, which otherwise was unlimited.

No further report of the British battle fleet's whereabouts had yet been received since that from the submarine I58 in the early hours of the morning. Presuming that their destination was Singapore—and there appeared to be nothing to divert their attention en route—and that the submarine's estimation of the ships' speed was correct, the battle fleet should by 9 am be some eighty miles west of the Anambas Islands. The search had therefore been concentrated in this area, with wide sweeps spreading out south, east and west to cover possible deceptive or evasive movements by the enemy.

All through the morning the ether was congested with radio messages between flight, squadron and corps commanders exchanging their views and reporting their position. These became increasingly anxious in tone as the hours passed with no sign of the British warships and only occasional false alarms to add to the strain. By 10.30 am several of the squadrons had probed so far that even Singapore was behind them, clearly visible eighty miles distant, and they had well exceeded their maximum range.

At 9.50 am there had been a moment of excitement

among the aircrews, by then well scattered over the South China Sea, when the third Genzan squadron of bombers had reported an enemy warship beneath her. A few seconds later came the message that they were attacking; then that bombs had been dropped; and finally that the vessel was only a minesweeper. The ship was, in fact, the *Tenedos*, making best speed back to Singapore after transmitting Phillips's message to Palliser earlier in the morning. The little destroyer, survivor from the First World War and ill-equipped for the second, evaded every one of the Genzan squadron's 600 kg. bombs, and completed her mission safely.

By 11.00 am all ninety-five aircraft of the 22nd Air Flotilla were on their return leg, with fuel gauges registering well below the half level, and with hopes of finding the battle fleet almost abandoned. Many of the crews, in fact, were preoccupied with endurance calculations rather than the enemy, and several squadrons had determined to set course for Kota Bharu rather than risk the longer sea passage to Cape Cambodia. Then at approximately 11.05 am Ensign Hoashi in one of the "Babs" reconnaissance aircraft, on the last leg of his sector search, caught sight of several unidentifiable vessels between a gap in the clouds. At once he swung to starboard, reduced height, and when he was in a more favourable position sent out a general call: "Sighted two enemy battleships seventy nautical miles south-east Kuantan course south-east."

The identity of the aircraft that had shadowed Force Z five hours earlier at dawn has never been made clear. Perhaps it was an army machine from Kota Bharu or a seaplane patrolling far to the south before returning to its cruiser. Like those from the naval reconnaissance aircraft of the previous evening, any report it may have transmitted of the British Fleet's whereabouts failed to reach Saigon. Until the sighting report soon after 11.00 am, Admiral Matsunaga had continued to base his calculations, and the orders to his commanders, on the submarine's night-time message; and his squadrons had cruised far south beyond their range because I58's commander estimated Force Z's course as southerly instead of south-westerly. In the alarm and confusion of a sudden sighting in the dark of a battle fleet bearing down at high speed, the mistake was understandable. It was only one of a number of minor errors, miscalculations and failures, that marked a pursuit and evasion in which the capacities of weary men were taxed to the limit by the bewildering magnitude of their task and the very complexity and limitations of their own technical aids. From dawn on the previous day the pressures of fortune and misfortune had fallen and risen again almost hourly for each side in the hunt, compromising wise judgments and cancelling out miscalculations; until at the most critical moment of the hunt one machine searching over that vast area of ocean, its mission almost abandoned, found itself just within sight of its quarry.

The train of events that led Force Z to Kuantan were beyond the calculation of the most far-sighted commander; the decision to leave the coast again and venture back in the very direction of the dangers from which the ships had been fleeing was boldly intended. It also proved fatal.

Admiral Phillips had brought Force Z off Kuantan at 8.00 am, preceded by one of his own Walrus amphibians which had been catapulted off on an anti-submarine and reconnaissance patrol. There was no sign of any activity, and this was confirmed by the crew of the Walrus. Shortly afterwards, the commander of the destroyer *Express*, which had been sent into the harbour to investigate, signalled by Aldis lamp to the flagship: "All's as quiet as a wet Sunday afternoon." The battle fleet continued its southerly course, passing down inside the seven-fathom shoal ten miles from the coast. The palm-fringed shoreline, with its silver-brown sands, and the off-shore islands, appeared quite deserted.

The signal from Singapore of a landing in this area was obviously based on false information, perhaps on the evidence of an over-imaginative or weary shore lookout. Or it might, Phillips calculated, have been based on an advance Intelligence report that had incorrectly judged the time of the invasion. Credence was added to this theory by the sighting, some four hours earlier at first light, of what appeared to be a junk or barge towing a number of smaller craft. In his eagerness to reach Kuantan as quickly as possible, Phillips had not allowed himself to be diverted by these at the time, but when it was agreed that the vessels might have been motor landing craft acting as the spearhead of the invasion, and Captain Tennant signalled suggesting that they might now be investigated, the C in C ordered the battle fleet back on to a north-easterly course. His own aerial reconnaissance had revealed no sign of enemy warships in the vicinity; he was now within range of shore-based fighters as cover, and was some 500 miles distant from the Saigon airfields, of which he had so often been warned by his Chief of Staff in Singapore. Admiral

Phillips recognised that the likelihood of his intercepting a major invasion of Kuantan was slight, but considered that it was worth exploring now that the degree of risk from air and surface attack had been so reduced.

The surprise and alarm, when, half an hour later, *Tenedos*, now far to the south of the main force, reported herself under bombing attack, were therefore all the greater. First degree of readiness was at once ordered for the high-angle guns. One of the *Repulse*'s Walrus machines was catapulted off on reconnaissance, and it banked away to the north, climbing laboriously. The intention of investigating the barges was abandoned. Course was altered first to 095 degrees and then to 135 degrees, speed increased to 20 and then to 25 knots. Once again the most rapid return to base was demanded by the change of circumstances.

The temperature had risen quickly during the last two hours as the sun climbed and the clouds thinned out to scattered flecks of cumulus. The crews in their flash hoods manning the Oerlikons, the multiple Vickers machine-guns and the eight-barrel pom-poms, were now unable to seek shade and were feeling the heat badly. Some of them were playing cards or talking together; others were staring out to sea or up into the steel-blue sky. The *Prince of Wales* and *Repulse* were in quarter line formation, the flagship leading, the three remaining destroyers in anti-submarine formation ahead and on either flank. The sea was smooth and the big ships were scarcely rolling.

The "Babs" reconnaissance aircraft was sighted by Force Z as a faint "blip" on the *Repulse*'s radar, some minutes before visual contact was made. At once an announcement was made over the battle cruiser's loudspeaker system: "Enemy aircraft in sight—action stations." The "Babs" was glimpsed briefly, a minute dot like some fragment of germ bacteria on the vast saucer of the sky. The guns ignored it. It was far out of range, summoning to their target a big force that was already smearing the radar screens on a 70 degree bearing.

The enemy was in sight on the starboard bow at 11.13 am: nine twin-engined Mihoro machines flying steadily at a great height in tight line-abreast formation. They turned slightly as they approached, to bring themselves dead ahead and over the *Repulse*, and at the same moment the *Prince of Wales*'s starboard 5.25-inch guns opened up, violating the ocean's peace with their staccato cannonade. The *Repulse*'s heavy high-angle armament joined in, then the destroyers', and, like a clean ceiling wantonly sprayed, the spots in their multitudes spattered the sky about the raiders: black and intense with a tiny golden core at the evil moment of explosion, then spreading and fading astern of the machines. The barrage multiplied, and with it the hectic sparkle of muzzle-flashes springing almost from stem to stern of the big ships. The line of aircraft continued their advance, as impervious as guardsmen to a holocaust, the ear-splitting cacophony from the guns a mockery of their powers of destruction.

The bombs fell simultaneously from the nine machines. Their moment of release was anticipated and calculated by hundreds aboard the ships. When they became visible, the men of the *Repulse* could see them best, arching down towards them as ever-growing dark globules, ignored only by the gunners whose asbestos hoods were already staining dark with sweat as they pumped their shells up two miles into the hot sky.

Tennant had seen fiercer bombing than this at Dunkirk; no one present had ever before seen such accurate bombing. Of the nine bombs that fell, one from each aircraft, seven exploded in the water very close to the port side of the *Repulse*, one just missed the starboard side of the ship, spraying those on deck with its tall geyser, and one struck amidships. This bomb tore through the hangar, leaving a fifteen-inch hole, and exploded on the armoured deck below in the Marines' mess. Grey smoke and fragments of metal, followed by a flash of flame, soared up into the sky.

The bombers flew on undisturbed in their immaculate formation.

Men below had been killed by the explosion. The stretcher parties were running through the smoke and stokers were emerging from it, nursing their wounds and seeking first aid. The catapult had been crippled, and the amphibian aircraft on it was tilted over at a sharp angle. It could never be flown now, and the bearded New Zealand pilot was struggling in the smoke to work his plane free and over the side before its fuel tanks exploded in the heat. The damage control parties had the hoses run out and were pouring sea water into the blaze. They had it under control within ten minutes, and the *Repulse* steamed on at twenty-five knots, her fighting efficiency unaffected.

The gun crews had not moved from their weapons. They were smoking cigarettes, wiping the sweat from their faces, kicking aside the hot piles of shell cases, placing ready new ammunition. No one believed this was the end of it.

The torpedo planes were late. They should have come in while the gun crews were still distracted by the high-level bombers and the immediate effect of their attack. The *Prince of Wales*'s radar picked them up on the screen at 11.30. Like the high-level bombers, they came in on the starboard bow, travelling fast in a glide and out of accurate range even of the 5.25s. There were about sixteen

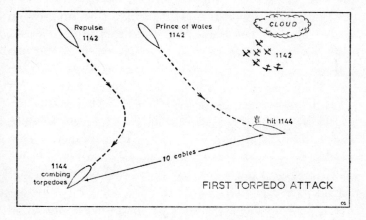

FIRST TORPEDO ATTACK

or seventeen of them in two groups, and they flew ahead of the ships from starboard to port and disappeared behind a small bank of cloud at about 3000 feet. The cloud concealed them for what seemed an unnatural length of time, as if the pilots were collecting their courage or deliberately tightening the suspense. Then they came out at 11.42 in loose groups of two or three, diving towards the port side of the *Prince of Wales*, at full speed.

Bugles blared on the two big ships, and the loudspeakers were calling out, "Stand by for barrage!" Every gun that could be brought to bear opened up, the machine-gun tracers streaming wide white arcs through the light puff marks of thousands of two-pound shells and the big grey balls from the heavier guns. Survival appeared impossible. This was the vaunted solid wall of steel and high explosive, the curtain of death, in reality. The gun crews were firing skilfully and accurately as they broke off to follow individual planes, that jinked and banked and twisted lower, and then suddenly steadied on course as if, after all, unperturbed by the hail of fire around them that continued to rip through wings and fuselage. Some aimed at the flagship, released their long projectiles while still at full speed and at 500 feet or higher, so that it seemed as if they must be torn apart on impact with the water. But the torpedoes winged down steadily, splashed in and held their shallow course at over 40 knots like racing swimmers at the start, trailing a line of delicate white foam towards the *Prince of Wales*. Others banked clear of the flagship with their bellies still loaded, and made for the battle cruiser.

Captain Tennant on the *Repulse*'s bridge saw them coming and waited. The fire below was almost out; only a thin stream of steam and smoke drifted astern. Every gun was firing, and the pom-pom crews were swinging their great eight-barrel weapons to and fro on their mountings to catch the profusion of targets at their most vulnerable moment. The paint on the shields was rising in blisters from the friction heat of hundreds of shells a minute.

When the planes steadied Tennant called out, "Turn 45 degrees to starboard," to the Navigating Officer, who passed the order to the Quartermaster in the upper conning tower, and at once the big ship began to heel over on the turn so that the men at the guns had to steady

themselves. One of the planes was on fire. It blazed up
in an orange and yellow ball for no more than a second
and scattered itself into a thousand pieces that joined the
splashes of shell fragments in the torn-up water. Another
flew slowly alongside the ship at a few hundred feet as if
challenging the gunners to simple target practice. It was
losing height in a gentle glide, and the tracers cut it to
pieces indelicately. It exploded like an impact-fused shell
as it hit the sea.

The other planes, relieved at last of their burden, pulled
up over the ship and the air gunners fired back in passing
at the clustered gun crews, some of whom twisted over
and fell limply to the deck. The Walrus pilot, who was
still astride his jammed machine, emptied the chambers of
his revolver at one plane that flashed low above his head.

The *Repulse* completed her turn away to comb the tracks
of the dozen or more torpedoes racing towards her. She
offered them only her stern, and the torpedoes passed by
harmlessly on either side and soon were gone.

Ten cables away the flagship was beginning to turn to
port as if to meet her torpedoes head on. She was too late.
Tennant saw the huge column of water rising from her
stern and the black smoke that followed it and drifted
away. At once the *Prince of Wales* listed 13 degrees
to port and lost 10 knots of speed. The blow she had
been struck was as deadly as that which had sealed the
fate of the *Bismarck* seven months earlier, and of Spanner's
whole mythical British Fleet in his prophetic romance.
Even Sir Eustace Tennyson d'Eyncourt, the late Director
of Naval Construction, had discovered no means of protecting a battleship's rudders and propellers—their Achilles'

heel, as he described them. Two torpedoes had struck this one vulnerable spot simultaneously: had crippled the rudder, jammed the port propeller shafts, sheering one of them so that it tore open a hole in the hull and, relieved suddenly of its propeller's resistance, caused its turbines to race themselves to frenzied ruination. Amid the turbulence of water pouring in under the pressure of the battleship's speed, half the ship's machinery was destroyed, and with it her ability to steer, and to fire her after heavy anti-aircraft guns. One double blow had lost the *Prince of Wales* her ability to turn and evade, and half her defences, so that she continued to steam helplessly to port, heeling over from the weight of water in her bowels. Up went her "not under control" balls, an ominous portent of annihilation that was observed with dismay from the bridge of the *Repulse*.

Captain Tennant could not understand what had happened to the RAF fighters. He already accepted that neither ship was likely to survive further torpedo attacks as determined and skilful as the first. But even half a dozen Buffaloes, sweeping among the "Nells" and "Bettys." might at least sufficiently distract the Japanese air crews and break up their runs, allowing his own ship to escape south. Tennant was beginning to feel disquiet about the state of his flagship's communications. Signals inquiring about the *Repulse*'s damage and describing her own were being transmitted only by Aldis lamp, and even these were disjointed and uncertain. It was clear that the internal damage to the *Prince of Wales* was serious, that she was no longer able to report progress of the battle to Singapore by wireless, and that this duty was now Tennant's.

During the brief lull that followed the torpedo attack,

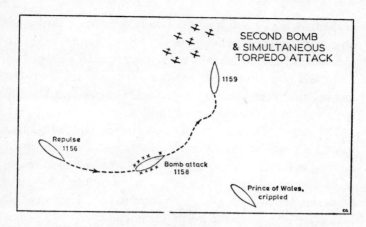

SECOND BOMB
& SIMULTANEOUS
TORPEDO ATTACK

1159

Repulse
1156

Bomb attack
1158

Prince of Wales,
crippled

Tennant therefore called for a report from his Chief Yeoman of Signals on what messages had been sent earlier to Admiral Palliser. He was horrified to learn that none at all had been picked up by his ship's wireless, although now almost an hour had passed since the first hostile radar sightings: long enough for the fighters to take off from Singapore and reach them. Tennant at once made on his own initiative an emergency signal to base, "Enemy aircraft bombing," and giving their position, following this with a more detailed four-line cypher signal.

This fuller account never reached Singapore. The tempo of the attacks was reaching a crescendo as the rest of the 22nd Air Flotilla's squadrons hastened to join battle. A squadron of bombers from the Mihoro corps and nine more Genzan torpedo planes arrived in the target area together to carry out a perfectly co-ordinated attack. A few minutes before twelve o'clock the Mihoro bombers swept in high from the south, again concentrating on the *Repulse*, and repeated the same immaculate performance as the first, every bomb falling within a hundred yards and obscuring the ship behind a solid screen of geysers. The old battle cruiser came out with water flooding from her decks and most of the gun crews soaked through. Tennant had ordered port helm as an evasion, and she was heeling hard over in her swing round to north.

The bridge personnel were ready for the Genzan planes, too. They were doing magnificent work, calling out crisply above the sound of the guns the bearing, height and range of every plane, and Tennant was manœuvring the big ship as if she were some whippy motor boat. The torpedo planes came in from the north again, and the loudspeakers called the gun crews to switch their targets the moment they were in range.

The *Repulse*'s bows came round just in time to comb through the new tracks that swept in towards her like formating sharks and passed by on either side at a combined speed of some eighty miles an hour. Again there was the remarkable demonstration of survival by the big twin-engined machines that during the moment of dropping gave a sitting head-on target to every one of the battle cruiser's guns. These were pouring out shells at the rate of hundreds a second; but one after another they came steadily on, uncannily impervious to the splinters and bullets at point-blank range, until their apparent invulnerability was suddenly shattered. One of the Vickers's machine-gun crews caught a "Nell" in the full cone of its concentrated spray, and the plane fell to pieces before their eyes. It was just no longer there. Even the fragments and the crew seemed to dissolve to nothing in the holocaust of spray and smoke and flying metal that had spread about the ship.

By 12.00 the attack was over, and Tennant was able to give some attention to the state of his flagship, which was giving him increasing cause for concern. The *Prince of Wales* was still wallowing awkwardly through the water far to the south of the *Repulse*, incapable of evasion and, judged by the weakness of her last barrage, scarcely able to defend herself. Tennant therefore turned his ship through 180 degrees and closed his flagship at reduced speed so that he could better examine for himself her damage and perhaps give her assistance. At the same time he signalled by lamp, "Thanks to Providence have so far dodged nineteen torpedoes." There was no reply. It seemed as if *Prince of Wales*, like a dying man, was too preoccupied with her own wounds and imminent end to give thought to anything else.

A sense of detachment from the savage events taking place so close to the flagship had taken possession of those members of the crew of the *Prince of Wales* who were able to watch the battle. Crippled since the first torpedo strike, they could only observe with admiration the defiant efforts of the older and lesser ship to protect herself. The feeling of helplessness and failure was hard to bear. They had been defeated by the guns of the Germans earlier in the year; now it seemed, inevitably and in the enemy's own time, they were to go down under a swarm of Japanese torpedoes. It had looked as if the planes intended to finish off the *Repulse* first. This seemed to be confirmed when at 12.20, while the two ships were some four cables apart, yet another attack developed from the south. There were nine planes, approaching low and breaking into the now familiar loose echelon pattern. But this time, while at about three miles, range, the squadron divided in two, one formation of three swinging to the left towards the *Repulse* and the other six maintaining their course towards the crippled *Prince of Wales*. Again Tennant brought his ship round towards the attack, and when the torpedoes dropped at 12.21 he hoped that once more he would evade them. The three trails were already racing towards his bows when he turned to watch the development of the attack on his flagship.

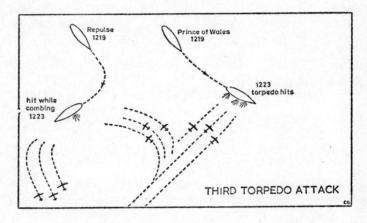

One of these planes was abaft the *Repulse*'s beam and about to drop its torpedo. Then Tennant saw it suddenly tip its wings almost to the vertical and turn towards his own ship, followed by two more of the group. The torpedoes fell from the "Nells'" bellies almost at once and Tennant could watch them, dark and running shallow and true, knowing that if he swung to avoid them he would receive the full brunt of the three torpedoes he was already combing.

Tennant saw that one was certain to hit. His voice came

over the loudspeakers "Stand by for torpedo!" and he
watched it, with the other officers on the bridge at his side,
for the full length of its course. It took ninety seconds to
reach the ship. It struck them square amidships, its explosion
lost in the medley of the guns' roar, sending a slight shudder
through the length of the *Repulse*. At once she began
listing to port. But she had stood the blow well. She still
had all her faculties and could steam at 25 knots. The
New Zealander at last succeeded in dragging free his
Walrus, and with the aid of a group of ratings dropped it
over the side. It rapidly fell astern, and then disappeared
in the battle cruiser's wake, to join the Japanese planes on
the sea bed.

It had taken the distant Japanese squadrons more than
an hour to reach the scene of battle. Some had been on
their return leg to Saigon, and they had turned and flown
south again at quarter throttle, torn between fear of missing
the kill and of running out of fuel. They were spurred on
by the voice of Ensign Hoashi, who, like some impresario
at a triumphant first night, was continuing to circle the
scene of battle to regale the absent pilots with an excited
commentary over the radio. Back in Saigon, Matsunaga
had raced out to one of the airfields and was standing by to
lead personally the reserve force of "Nells" in a final attack
if one or both capital ships survived and attempted to
escape. Soon after 12.30 he knew he would not be needed.

The *Repulse*'s end came with terrifying suddenness. Three
more uncommitted squadrons were in the vicinity ready
to go in, and the leader of one of these, who had observed
the success of the battle cruiser's evasive tactics and the hit

made as a result of the unorthodoxy of the last attack, ordered his pilots to split and dive in from all directions. The *Repulse*'s Air Defence Officer at once recognised the impossibility of meeting all these attacks simultaneously, and could only direct the gun-layers to concentrate on the aircraft before they dropped, and disregard the nearer and more tempting targets that roared empty over or close to the ship.

Soon every gun was again firing. Some of the dead crew were lying nearby; others had been removed. The water in the pom-poms' cooling jackets was boiling furiously. A "Betty" disintegrated, and its fuel momentarily flared into a deep red ball before the pieces fell like a hurled handful of pebbles into the sea.

At 12.25 there were at least eight trails speeding like ruled white lines on the blue sea towards the *Repulse*, and all that Tennant could do was to manœuvre his ship to avoid as many of these as possible. In spite of her earlier damage, the ship answered well to the helm. The Quartermaster brought the ship swerving round to port, and then before the turn was completed, hard back on the opposite course, leaving behind a tortuous death signature of white foam.

The first torpedo struck her on the port side abreast of the gun room, sending up a great fountain of spray and jamming the rudder. It didn't matter. Further evolutions were in any case futile. Almost at the same moment three more crashed against her side, two to port and one to starboard. The successive shock waves raced from end to end of the *Repulse*'s hull, causing her to list first one way and then the other.

Captain Tennant knew that his old ship could not survive

these successive wounds, and that the end was near. "Everybody on deck. Prepare to abandon ship. Clear away Carley floats," came over the loudspeaker system, which mercifully continued to work over almost all the ship. This was at once followed by an order for everyone to come up from below. The ship had settled hard to port, the angle increasing rapidly, but she was still making 15 knots. Men were running up gangways and along passageways and decks that had suddenly assumed ominous angles. They moved rapidly, determinedly, without panic or despair. Most of them were in rubber-soled shoes, and there was little noise. The guns were silent. Disciplined self-survival ruled the ship, which shuddered once or twice as she lost her speed and suffered the failure of one more vast and vital component, far below. Everywhere in her bowels things were breaking and the temperate equatorial waters pouring in, flushing away her mighty strength.

Four men were carrying on a stretcher an officer accidentally wounded before the action. They tied two lifebelts to him and hurled him into the water thirty feet below. The walking wounded were making their way up hesitantly from the sick bay, some with a man at either elbow. High above, several figures detached themselves from the air defence positions on the masts and fell, with limbs moving in slow defiance, ninety feet into the sea. Two of them misjudged their distance and broke up their bodies on the sloping steel decks far below.

Captain Tennant remained on the bridge. Four minutes had passed since his ship had received her death blows. She had three more minutes. There were two or three hundred men on the forecastle below him. They were passive, unkempt and expectant, still awaiting the word from their captain. Commander Dendy and other officers were among them. Tennant held the rails against the 40 degree list with one hand, and putting a megaphone to his mouth with the other, called down to them, "You've put up a good show. Now look after yourselves and God bless you."

When the *Repulse* was at 60 degrees they could walk up the deck and slide down her side. It was too late to launch boats, and about six hundred men were doing this. The dark camouflage-painted side was like a shelving beach packed with exploratory swimmers. The water was still and calm, already streaked with foul fuel oil, warmly uninviting. Only litter and a few Carley floats gave hope of sustenance.

Many of the men slid on their buttocks. The ship's underside was coated with a foul slippery compound of fuel oil and weed, and they at once lost control, sliding wildly towards the sea, striking violently, and breaking their ankles or their spines against the ship's bilge keel. Others waited until she was over to 70 degrees and ran clumsily in their blown-up lifebelts, over her deep scarlet bottom, and into the water. Those who could, swam strongly away, sparing an anxious glance upwards for the expected machine-gun attack. There were shouts from the weaker ones, and some cheering responses. Hardly a man escaped from the soft spreading embrace of the stinking oil that weighed them down, lapped foully against their faces, and choked their noses and throats. Many of those who had injured themselves against the bilge keel were the first to go.

The *Repulse* hung at 70 degrees for a minute and a half, and went down stern first, and with astonishing grace and silence, at twenty-seven minutes to one. Tennant was still aboard. He had moved down to B gun deck, better to enter the water, when the sea came up rapidly to meet him. He let it come; there was nothing for him to do. His ship turned right over on him, and he was at once drawn into the blackness of her death and taken far down on her turbulent descent to the bottom. Tennant wondered whether he should take one deep swallow in an effort to hasten the end. But he held on and saw the black change to dark green, then to light green as he swiftly rose again above his ship that had so miraculously allowed him to live. Something hit him hard on the head, and he was made nearly insensible in spite of the protection of his tin helmet. Soon after he surfaced, he heard a voice calling, "Here you are, sir." Men who had at once recognised him were leaning from the edge of a Carley float and dragging him on board.

In the last divided torpedo attack all the three aircraft that had continued on course towards the *Prince of Wales* had hit their target. They could scarcely have failed. The flagship's speed was less than 15 knots, she could not turn, and only a few of her guns were still firing. The three torpedoes struck almost simultaneously, well spaced out on the battleship's starboard side near the stem, abreast of the second 14-inch gun turret, and aft. As the water poured in the ship almost righted herself, and this balancing of her list made her appear less crippled than she had been. Certainly from the *Prince of Wales* the plight of the *Repulse* looked more critical, and Phillips ordered two of his destroyers to her aid and to pick up survivors if she went down. He then made ready for his flagship's new ordeal, for even now the Japanese had not exhausted their strength.

The battle closed as it had opened, with a high-level attack: nine bombers neatly abreast coming in from the south slowly above the scattered clouds. They crossed the flagship from port to starboard as she steamed heavily north, burdened by thousands of tons of water, at eight knots. Six of the flagship's operative 5.25s opened up, carelessly sprinkling the sky with black puffs. The bombers did not seem to care.

Admiral Phillips and his staff officers, with John Leach at their side, stood on the *Prince of Wales*'s compass platform in their tin helmets and counted the bombs as they came down, one from each aircraft. At the last second the captain called out, "Now!" and they all fell flat to the deck. Again the accuracy was devastating. The pattern fell aft, hurling fragments of steel with the waterspouts from near misses high in the air, and one stray struck amidships on the port side of the main deck, causing a fire. Men died in the hot twisted metal, amid the battle scent of explosive, and lay uncared for in the sun. The stretcher parties ran awkwardly among the debris, pausing with morphia needles and tourniquets.

Captain Leach called up the destroyer *Express* to take off the wounded, and her captain, Lieutenant-Commander F. J. Cartwright, had her hard alongside by 1.05. Leach was reluctant to accept that the end was near. He was still trying vainly to call up for tugs from Singapore to help them back. But those last torpedoes had torn out the great ship's heart; and the bombs had been only vicious shots into her corpse. The reports continued to come in to him telling of the devastation below, and within five minutes the captain had recognised the inevitable, and gave the order to abandon ship.

Ten minutes remained for fifteen hundred men to jump, or scramble by ropes and nets, down on to the deck of the destroyer hugging the starboard side of the battleship's forecastle. It was a disorderly, hectic abandonment in which the discipline was always strained but never finally broke. Some who despaired of reaching the front of the groups packed along the sides blew up their lifebelts and leaped into the water to swim to the Carley floats. There were many others trapped below whose cries of despair rose in a last agonised chorus from the quarter-deck ventilators.

Just before 1.20 pm the *Prince of Wales* shuddered once more and began to roll ponderously to port. Her starboard bilge keel rose and knocked against the delicate hull of the *Express*. She tilted as the keel rose higher, and almost capsized with her great load of survivors, packed below and milling, elbow to elbow, on her decks. For a moment it seemed as if she must go. Cartwright had the destroyer going astern. Skilfully he dragged her free from the slowly rotating grasp of the huge hull, the last men scrambling frantically overboard, and the mountains of water that suddenly erupted between the battleship and the little *Express*.

The *Prince of Wales* turned turtle with mighty grandeur, extinguishing her last fires in the ocean and concealing her wounds beneath her great red belly. Then she disappeared into the centre of her own fuel oil.

Flight-Lieutenant T. A Vigors, Officer Commanding 453 Squadron, was the first on the scene. He led in four more Brewster Buffaloes from Singapore at about 1.18 pm. The flight flew north in pursuit of the last "Nell" bombers that were hovering on the horizon in case they might still be needed, and had returned when he saw them jettison their bombs and make off at a higher speed than he could match. One battleship, bottom up, was all that remained of the big ships; and that, too, disappeared as he flew low over it.

The Buffaloes flew low over the *Vampire* and *Electra* as they worked their way slowly along the wide lane of oil slick dragging black, exhausted men on to their decks, then raced over the packed decks of the *Express*, engaged on similar work to the north. There was nothing the pilots could do except, perhaps, to show by their presence their sympathy, and to encourage the rescuers. Tennant's signal informing his base that Force Z was being attacked had been received at 12.04. The Buffaloes had taken off eleven minutes later from Kallang airfield, and had taken little over an hour for their flight. Vigors's report describing the cheerful waves of the survivors from the water was later widely publicised, and it has since been claimed that the men were in fact shaking their fists in anger. From Captain Tennant's own observation from the bridge of the destroyer *Vampire*, as she picked her way tenderly through the Carley floats and wreckage, it appears more likely that everyone was too preoccupied with the rescue work or their own survival to spare the Buffaloes more than a passing glance.

The *Express* left the scene at 2.15, without room aboard for another survivor. At that time all who were still alive were safely on rafts or in the *Vampire* or *Electra*, which collected these remaining men until 4 pm. Between them they numbered ninety officers and 1195 men from the *Prince of Wales*'s total complement of 110 officers and 1502 men; and forty-two officers and 754 men from the *Repulse*'s sixty-nine officers and 1240 men. Forty-seven officers and 793 men had either gone down in their ships, died after their rescue, or perished in the suffocating oil-laden waters of the South China Sea. The remainder were carried carefully, uncomfortably, on the burning hot decks of the destroyers, or below where the air was heavy with the scent of chloroform and fuel oil and endlessly-brewing tea.

They arrived back at their base just before midnight, and those who could do so made their way over narrow gangways and through tropical rain in the black-out to a big shed. There they queued for tea from giant urns, many still black and sick with the oil, and joked with those they recognised, and counted off, casually and mostly without rancour, those they had lost.

Sir Winston Churchill has told how he convened a meeting, "mostly Admiralty," in the Cabinet War Room on 9 December at 10 pm to discuss what should be done with the *Prince of Wales* and *Repulse*. After some conversation, it was thought to be too late to reach a final decision that night, and it was agreed "to sleep on it." While the meeting broke up, Force Z was racing towards Kuantan at dawn, distantly followed by Japanese reconnaissance aircraft, and the first machines of the 22nd Air Flotilla were taking off near Saigon.

Churchill has also told of his awakening the following morning, and of the telephone ringing at his bedside. The voice over the line was that of Sir Dudley Pound, speaking so incoherently that the Prime Minister could not at first understand him. ". . . I have to report to you that the *Prince of Wales* and the *Repulse* have both been sunk by aircraft. Tom Phillips is drowned." There was no doubt about the truth of the report, the First Sea Lord added.

"As I turned over and twisted in bed the full horror of the news sank in on me," Churchill has written.[22] His distress is understandable. He, and he alone, had been finally responsible for sending the battle fleet to Singapore at this dangerous time, and against the strong pleas of those whose task it was to manage Britain's maritime affairs. He had selected the ships, and even the Commander-in-Chief. If direct blame for the catastrophe has to be attached to one man, then Winston Churchill must accept it.

But it is wise to look more deeply, and distantly, too. It is worth taking into account, for example, the difficulties faced by service departments which have to select their priorities in peace time. It is difficult to be bold and sweeping, to throw away your old and well-tried weapons and replace them with the new and revolutionary. Except in the crisis of war, the military mind is not conditioned to such practices; nor is it encouraged to do so by the parsimonious offerings of a nation at peace. It is the people themselves, subject to the hopeful, fumbling, imperfect workings of democracy, who are finally responsible for their own defence. They, understandably and invariably, demand security at the lowest possible cost. They will accept almost any weapon offered to them so long as it offers reassurance, adds to their own self-conceit and the fear of their enemies, and does not conflict with their ethical standards—however curious these may be. The swift, streamlined fighter was a clean, sporting weapon, for example, but there was no interest in torpedo planes, and the public flinched from the possession of a great bomber fleet in peace time. It is fruitless now to calculate that a powerful force of the most modern torpedo bombers stationed in Malaya could have crushed the Japanese invasion, and that they would have cost far less to build, and maintain over the years, than the two capital ships that went down after destroying four per cent of the enemy. Before the war, the British people would never have permitted the disposal of their battle fleet. But they would have done well to examine more closely the integrity and the nature of the ambitions of some of their politicians.

No one has ever questioned the need for Admiral Phillips, under the tactical and moral circumstances of the time, to leave Singapore and challenge the enemy. Some authorities felt that he should have turned back, and left at once for the safety of the Indian Ocean, as soon as he was certain that he would not get fighter cover at Singora. Sir Dudley Pound, and many others who accepted Phillips's need to reconnoitre Kuantan, believed he should not have allowed himself to be diverted back north-east again. No one has ever been able to explain satisfactorily why he did not call for fighter cover on 10 December when he knew he was likely to be attacked, or even after the attack began. Pound thought he may have been influenced by the fact that he was some 400 miles from the Japanese land-based heavy machines, and that the fighter support the RAF in Singapore could offer was in any case so slight as to be of little value. It was Phillips's misfortune that the communications of his flagship were damaged within seconds of the first torpedo attack, so that any call for help he may have sent later never got through.

The events of 10 December, 1941, must be seen in the light of what we know of Admiral Phillips, his character, his regard for the power of his own weapons, and of those of the enemy. We now know that the destructive power of anti-aircraft guns was everywhere over-estimated in 1941, that the *matériel* and skill of the Japanese air arm—and especially of their aircraft and torpedoes—was everywhere underestimated. Phillips miscalculated the numbers, speed and range of the planes of the 22nd Air Flotilla, the accuracy and explosive power of its torpedoes. This was partly due to the absence of information, and partly due to the confidence he possessed in himself, and the weapons at his command.

Phillips turned back when he did because he estimated that the risks of persisting had become intolerable. He feared air attack because of the damage it might commit; he feared surface and submarine attack because, under the handicap of torpedo damage, he would be at a dangerous disadvantage. Above all, he knew that British maritime striking power in Eastern waters rested on his force alone. If Force Z went to the bottom, or was crippled, there was nothing of consequence left to carry on the fight.

The enigma of the whole operation lies in the C in C's failure to inform his base of his change of plan, and to request fighter cover at Kuantan. Ever since the North Sea engagements of the First World War, when the most serious indiscretions occurred on both sides through divulging a force's position by using the radio, "wireless silence" had become almost an obsession in the Royal Navy. Phillips judged that his change of plan at midnight did not justify taking the risk of revealing his position to the enemy. As his Chief of Staff ashore had given him the vital information about a new landing, and would appreciate Phillips's need to maintain wireless silence, Phillips presumed that Palliser knew he would make straight for Kuantan, and would accordingly provide Force Z with fighter cover. Admiral Palliser failed to do so. Moreover, he failed to inform his C in C that the Kuantan landing was based on unofficial information which had not been confirmed.

The extent to which a brilliant commander can expect standards of intelligence and speed of thinking to match his own is one of the imponderables of military conduct. This was not the first naval tragedy that was, in part, caused by the failure of a subordinate to meet the exceptional expectations of his senior. Military mediocrity must always spell disaster; wide disparity between the intellects of senior officers will also sometimes result in catastrophe. This has always been an insoluble problem, and will remain so as long as services seek brilliant minds, and on the rare occasions when they acquire them, promote them to high command. Phillips's judgment of the insight of his Chief of Staff was also influenced by his own long experience in staff work, in which he had acquired an almost psychical perception of the reasoning and reactions of commanders at sea to new situations.

They found John Leach, floating face down in the water an hour after his ship went down. Tom Phillips was never seen again. His body lies somewhere near the rusting-away fragments of his Force Z. Death on that December afternoon, by oil fuel suffocation or entombment in the bowels of shattered ships, was fearful and squalid almost beyond imagination. But it was never ignoble. The historical fact that the annihilation of Force Z signalled the end of a maritime era is of little consequence, of purely parochial interest, compared with the way men, who were fated for defeat by misfortune and misjudgment, suffered and died, or survived with honour.

THE END

Sources Consulted

Acknowledgments

Index

Sources Consulted

BOOKS

21 ACKWORTH, Captain Bernard, *The Restoration of England's Sea Power* (1935)
   Britain in Danger (1937)
   Admiralty Battle Summary No. 14 (1954)
   ALTHAM, Captain E., *Jellicoe* (1938)
1 ARMSTRONG, Lt. G. E., *Torpedoes and Torpedo Vessels* (1896)
   ASH, Bernard, *Someone Had Blundered* (1960)
   ATTIWILL, Kenneth, *The Singapore Story* (1959)
   AUPHAN, Rear-Admiral P. and NORDAL, J., *The French Navy in World War II* (1959)
   BENNETT, Lt.-General H. Cordon, *Why Singapore Fell* (1945)
10 BOYLE, Andrew, *Trenchard* (1962)
   BROWN, Cecil, *Suez to Singapore* (1942)
8 BURLINGHAME, Roger, *General Billy Mitchell* (1952)
14 BYWATER, Hector C., *Sea Power in the Pacific* (1921)
   A Searchlight on the Navy (1934)
4 CHALMERS, Rear-Admiral W. S., *The Life and Letters of David Earl Beatty* (1951)
27 CHURCHILL, Winston S., *The Second World War* (Vol. 2, 1949)
22   *The Second World War* (Vol. 3, 1950)
   LAIRD CLOWES, Sir William, *The Royal Navy: A History* (1903)
   CRESWELL, Commander James, *Naval Warfare* (1936)
   DOMVILLE, Admiral Sir Barry, *Look to Your Moat* (1937)
   DOUHET, Giulio, *The Command of the Air* (1921)

Sources Consulted

25 DREYER, Admiral Sir Frederick, *The Sea Heritage* (1955)

6 FALLS, Cyril, *The First World War* (1960)

FRANKLIN, A. and G., *One Year of Life: The Story of H.M.S. Prince of Wales* (1944)

GALLACHER, O. D., *Retreat in the East* (1942)

GILMOUR, O. W., *Singapore to Freedom* (1943)

24 GRENFELL, Russell, *Main Fleet to Singapore* (1951)
Sea Power in the Next War (1938)
The Bismarck Episode (1948)

GROVES, General P. R. C., *Behind the Smoke Screen* (1934)

9 HOARE, Sir Samuel (Lord Templewood), *Empire of the Air* (1957)

HOUGH, R., *The Fleet that Had to Die* (1958)

HUIE, W. B., *The Fight for Air Power* (1942)

HUNTER, F. T., *Beatty, Jellicoe, Sims and Rodman* (1919)

HURREN, B. J., *Perchance: a Short History of British Naval Aviation* (1949)

JELLICOE, Admiral of the Fleet Lord, *The Grand Fleet* (1919)
The Crisis of the Naval War (1920)

JOUBERT DE LA FERTE, Air Chief Marshal Sir Philip, *Birds and Fishes* (1958)

KEMP, Lieutenant-Commander P. K., *Victory at Sea 1939-45* (1957)

KERR, Admiral Mark, *Land, Sea and Air* (1927)

KIRBY, Major-General S. Woodburn, *The War against Japan* (Vol. 1, 1957)

7 LEVINE, Isaac Don, *Flying Crusader* (1943)

20 LIDDELL HART, Captain B. H., *Europe in Arms* (1937)

3 MARDER (Ed.), Arthur J., *Fear God and Dread Nought: The Correspondence of Admiral of the Fleet Lord Fisher of Kilverstone* (Vols. 1-3, 1952-9)

23 *From the Dreadnought to Scapa Flow* (Vol. 1, 1961)

5 MORISON, E. E., *Admiral Sims and the Modern American Navy* (1942)

16 MORISON, S. E., *History of the United States Naval Operations in World War II: The Rising Sun in the Pacific* (1948)

OKUMIYA, M. and HORIKOSHI, J., with CUIDIN, N., *Zero!* (1957)

PARKES, Oscar, *British Battleships* (1958)

PERCIVAL, Lt.-General A. E., *The War in Malaya* (1949)

RALEIGH, Walter, *The War in the Air* (Vol. 1, 1922)

28 RICHARDS, D. and ST. GEORGE SAUNDERS, H., *Royal Air Force 1939-45* (1954)

RICHMOND, Admiral Sir Herbert, *Sea Power in the Modern World* (1934)

Economy and Naval Security (1931)

26 ROSKILL, Captain S. W., *The Strategy of Sea Power* (1962)

17   *The War at Sea* (Vol. 1, 1954)

SCOTT, Admiral Sir Percy, *Fifty Years in the Royal Navy* (1919)

DE SEVERSKY, A. *Air Power: Key to Survival* (1952)

SHERWOOD, Robert E., *The White House Papers of Harry L. Hopkins* (1948)

SLEEMAN, Lt. C. W., *Torpedoes and Torpedo Warfare* (1880)

SPANNER, E. F., *The Broken Trident* (1926)

The Naviators (1926)

11 SUETER, Rear-Admiral Murray F., *Airmen or Noahs* (1928)

TURNBULL, A. D. and LORD, C. L., *History of United States Naval Aviation* (1949)

12 WILSON, H. W., *Ironclads in Action* (1896)

Battleships in Action (1926)

15 YOKOTA, Y., *The Kaiten Weapon* (1962)

ANNUALS, PAMPHLETS, PERIODICALS, ETC.

Army, Navy and Air Force Gazette

Konnichi no Wadai, Tokio, July 1956

Hansard

Scientific American

Illustrated London News

2 *Brassey's Navy Annual*

Jane's Fighting Ships

Jane's All the World's Aircraft

Sources Consulted

13 *National Geographic Magazine*, July 1942
  London Gazette
  Admiralty Intelligence Pamphlets
  Saturday Evening Post
  Naval Operations Papers, Imperial Japanese Navy H.Q.
  United Services Review
19 Report of the Sub-Committee of the CID on the vulnerability
    of Capital Ships to Air Attack
  Newspapers published in London and New York

Acknowledgments

The author and publishers wish to thank the following Publishers, Authors, Executors and Trustees for permission to quote copyright material:

Captain B. H. Liddell Hart, *Europe in Arms*; A. J. Marder and Jonathan Cape Ltd., *Fear God and Dread Nought: the Correspondence of Admiral of the Fleet, Lord Fisher of Kilverstone*; Sir Isaac Pitman and Sons Ltd., *Airmen or Noahs* by Rear-Admiral Murray F. Sueter; Seeley, Service and Co. Ltd., *British Battleships* by Oscar Parkes; William Collins Sons and Co. Ltd., *Empire of the Air* by Lord Templewood, and *Trenchard* by Andrew Boyle; Cyril Falls and Longmans, Green & Co. Ltd., *The First World War*; G. Bell & Sons Ltd., *Sea Power in the Modern World* by Admiral Sir Herbert Richmond; Eyre & Spottiswoode Ltd., *The Restoration of England's Sea Power* by Captain Bernard Acworth; Ivor Nicolson & Watson Ltd., *Perchance: a Short History of British Naval Aviation* by B. J. Hurren; the Executors of Captain Russell Grenfell, and Faber and Faber Ltd., *Sea Power in the Next War*; Cassell & Co. Ltd., *The Second World War* by Sir Winston Churchill; The Houghton Miflin Co., *Admiral Sims and the Modern American Navy* by E. E. Morison; Rear-Admiral W. S. Chalmers and Hodder and Stoughton Ltd., *The Life and Letters of David Earl Beatty*; the Trustees of the Estate of Admiral Sir Frederick Dreyer, *The Sea Heritage*; the Controller of H. M. Stationery Office for Extracts from *Air Operations:* 2nd Report of the Prime Minister's Committee on Air Organisation and Home Defence Against Air Raids, 17th August, 1917, Memorandum of the position of

Acknowledgments

His Majesty's Government in the United Kingdom at the London Naval Conference 1930, Report of the Sub-Committee to the Committee of Imperial Defence on the Vulnerability of Capital Ships to Air Attack; *The War at Sea*, Vol. 1—The Defensive, by Captain S. W. Roskill, *History of the Royal Air Force* 1939-45, by D. Richards and H. St. George Saunders; The Admiralty Memorandum to the Prime Minister dated 28th August, 1941 on fleet dispositions in the Far East; Lord Brabazon of Tara for the extract from his speech in the House of Commons November 10th, 1936; The *Daily Telegraph* for the article by Winston Churchill in that newspaper September 1st, 1938; *The Times* for the extract from a leading article February 8th, 1930.

The extracts from *Flying Crusader* by Isaac Don Levine (Peter Davies Ltd.) are reprinted by permission of the original publisher Duell, Sloane and Pearce, New York. Copyright 1943, 1958 by Isaac Don Levine. The extracts from *General Billy Mitchell: Champion of Air Defence* by Roger Burlinghame, copyright 1952 McGraw-Hill Book Company Inc., are used by permission.

Index

251

Index

Index